LEISURE ARTS
PRESENTS

THE SPIRIT OF CHRISTMAS

CREATIVE HOLIDAY IDEAS

BOOK ELEVEN

Christmas is a time when we find our way back home, whether in person or in our hearts. It's a time to celebrate the birth of Jesus, relive childhood memories, continue cherished traditions, and share hospitality and goodwill with others. Of course, the center of this magical season is the hearth and home, where garlands are gaily strung, delicious aromas of home-baked treats waft through the air, and handmade presents are exchanged with excited anticipation. With this latest volume, you'll discover a sampling of good foods, delightful home decor, and wonderful gifts — all created to complement a variety of styles, from rustic country to elegant sophistication. May these merry offerings bring an abundance of holiday cheer to you and yours!

LEISURE ARTS, INC.
Little Rock, Arkansas

THE SPIRIT OF CHRISTMAS®
BOOK ELEVEN

"... and it was always said of him, that he knew how to keep Christmas well, if any man alive possessed the knowledge. May that be truly said of us, and all of us!"

— From *A Christmas Carol* by Charles Dickens

EDITORIAL STAFF

Vice President and Editor-in-Chief: Anne Van Wagner Childs
Executive Director: Sandra Graham Case
Editorial Director: Susan Frantz Wiles
Publications Director: Carla Bentley
Creative Art Director: Gloria Bearden
Senior Graphics Art Director: Melinda Stout

PRODUCTION

DESIGN
Design Director: Patricia Wallenfang Sowers
Designers: Katherine Prince Horton, Sandra Spotts Ritchie, Anne Pulliam Stocks, Linda Diehl Tiano, and Rebecca Sunwall Werle
Executive Assistant: Billie Steward

FOODS
Foods Editor: Celia Fahr Harkey, R.D.
Assistant Foods Editor: Jane Kenner Prather
Test Kitchen Home Economist: Rose Glass Klein
Test Kitchen Coordinator: Nora Faye Taylor
Test Kitchen Assistant: Susan Scott
Contributing Foods Editors: Susan Warren Reeves, R.D., and Kaye M. Beavers

TECHNICAL
Managing Editor: Kathy Rose Bradley
Senior Technical Writers: Briget Julia Laskowski and Margaret F. Cox
Technical Associates: Leslie Schick Gorrell and Kimberly J. Smith

EDITORIAL

Managing Editor: Linda L. Trimble
Associate Editor: Robyn Sheffield-Edwards
Assistant Editors: Tammi Williamson Bradley, Terri Leming Davidson, and Darla Burdette Kelsay
Copy Editor: Laura Lee Weland

ART
Book/Magazine Graphics Art Director: Diane M. Hugo
Senior Graphics Artist: Michael A. Spigner
Photography Stylists: Pam Choate, Sondra Daniel, Laura Dell, Karen Smart Hall, Aurora Huston, Courtney Frazier Jones, and Christina Tiano Myers

PROMOTIONS
Managing Editors: Tena Kelley Vaughn and Marjorie Ann Lacy
Associate Editors: Steven M. Cooper, Dixie L. Morris, and Jennifer Leigh Ertl
Designer: Dale Rowett
Art Director: Linda Lovette Smart
Production Artist: Leslie Loring Krebs
Publishing Systems Administrator: Cindy Lumpkin
Publishing Systems Assistant: Susan Mary Gray

BUSINESS STAFF

Publisher: Bruce Akin
Vice President, Marketing: Guy A. Crossley
Marketing Manager: Byron L. Taylor
Print Production Manager: Laura Lockhart
Vice President and General Manager: Thomas L. Carlisle
Retail Sales Director: Richard Tignor

Vice President, Retail Marketing: Pam Stebbins
Retail Marketing Director: Margaret Sweetin
Retail Customer Services Manager: Carolyn Pruss
General Merchandise Manager: Russ Barnett
Vice President, Finance: Tom Siebenmorgen
Distribution Director: Ed M. Strackbein

Library of Congress Catalog Card Number 97-71976
International Standard Book Number 0-8487-4150-1

TABLE OF CONTENTS

THE SIGHTS OF CHRISTMAS

Page 6

TABLE OF CONTENTS
(Continued)

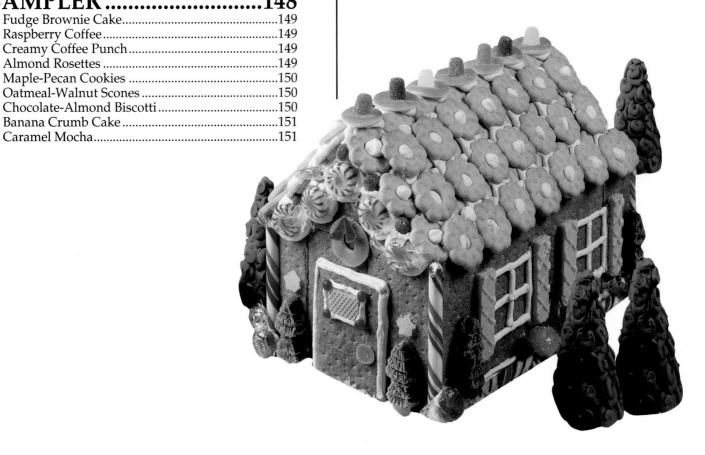

THE SIGHTS OF CHRISTMAS

Nothing can compare to the sights of Christmas — the warm glow of candles, a sparkling tree trimmed with glee, and wreaths wrapped with ribbons, baubles, and beads. From Santa's sweetshop to the holy Nativity, our festive decorating themes make it easy to enhance your traditional adornments or to create a whole new Yuletide look. Each endearing collection includes a treasury of unique holiday ornaments for the evergreen, as well as accents like tabletop topiaries, sweet stockings, and wall hangings for the home. May your holiday surroundings fill the season with merriment and joy!

SNOWY MOUNTAIN CHRISTMAS

You can re-create the feel of a rustic mountaintop retreat with this array of winter-inspired decorations. Dusted with powdery "snow," the evergreen is trimmed with Scandinavian touches such as cutwork snowflakes, miniature sleds, and felt mittens — all created in cheery red and white. A cozy throw pillow and coordinating lamp make relaxing by the fire to read a traditional Christmas story extra nice, and matching felt and flannel stockings continue the warm appeal. An ideal setting for nature enthusiasts, this alpine collection includes woodburned frames — great for displaying snowy-day photographs — and homemade candles featuring woodsy accents. Instructions for the projects shown here and on the following pages begin on page 14.

(*Opposite*) Decked with a sleighload of lodge-style trims, our **Snowy Mountain Christmas Tree** (*page 14*) features **Cutwork Snowflakes** (*page 14*), blanket-stitched **Mitten Ornaments** (*page 14*), miniature cross-stitched **Bellpulls** (*page 15*), and woodburned **Snapshot** and **Sled Ornaments** (*page 16*). A pair of antique child-size skis, little redbirds, and miniature old-fashioned lanterns complete the decorations.

Generous cuffs top cheery **Nordic Appliquéd Stockings** (*page 18*), which are made from coordinating fabrics.

Fashioned from layers of felt, our **Nordic Appliquéd Tree Skirt** (*page 16*) is graced with majestic reindeer, simple trees, and button-accented snowflakes.

(Opposite) Branded designs provide a rustic finish to **Wintry Woodburned Frames** *(page 19)*. To craft the coordinating **Covered Lamp** *(page 17)*, a padded lamp base is wrapped in flannel and tied with jute. The shade is dressed in red felt and embellished with a snowflake ornament.

Pinecones, greenery sprigs, and berries add a warm holiday glow to quaint **Ice Candles** *(page 19)*.

Felt appliqués, decorative stitches, and antique silver buttons accent a comfy **Rustic Throw Pillow** *(page 17)*.

SNOWY MOUNTAIN CHRISTMAS TREE

(Shown on page 9)

Outfitted in red and white and outdoor accents, this 8½-foot-tall pine tree celebrates a mountain lodge holiday.

Inspired by snow-covered slopes, we plumped the evergreen with flocked pine sprays and placed child-size antique skis in the tree. Among miniature lanterns that cover the lights, red bead and "ice crystal" garlands wind throughout the tall pine, and "icicle" and "snowball" ornaments dangle from the boughs. Crimson birds, toy skis, and a small log cabin placed atop the tree are perfect trimmings for an alpine playground.

Hand-crafted trims make the pine a winter treasure. Our Snapshot Ornaments (page 16) feature woodburned squares framing favorite images. The Sled Ornaments (page 16) are miniature wooden sleds with woodburned reindeer and painted trim. Other adornments on the tree include Bellpulls (page 15), which are quick decorations to cross stitch, and Cutwork Snowflakes (this page), showcasing intricate patterns. Use our simple two-layer appliqué method to stitch a flurry of flakes. Mitten Ornaments (this page) are easy to craft with felt shapes and hand stitching.

Completing our Christmas lodge scene is a cozy "woolen" tree skirt, cut from felt layers and embellished with Nordic appliqués and plaid flannel trim.

CUTWORK SNOWFLAKES

(Shown on page 10)

For each snowflake, you will need one 6" square each of red felt, ivory felt, and tracing paper; ivory thread; and small sharp scissors.

1. Trace grey and dark blue lines of snowflake A pattern onto tracing paper square.
2. Place felt squares together and center pattern on red felt square (back of ornament); pin layers together.
3. Beginning at center of pattern, use ivory thread and a short stitch length to sew squares together along grey lines of pattern. Trim threads close to stitching.
4. Cutting through all layers, cut out shape along dark blue lines of pattern. Carefully tear pattern from stitched lines.
5. Carefully cutting through ivory felt only and cutting close to stitched lines, use small scissors to trim away areas indicated by shading on pattern.

MITTEN ORNAMENTS

(Shown on page 10)

For each ornament, you will need ivory, red, and black felt; 7" of red yarn; 1 yd of black yarn; black embroidery floss; a large needle; ⅝" dia. red button; tracing paper; small sharp scissors; and fabric glue.

1. Trace mitten and cuff patterns onto tracing paper; cut out. Cut 2 mittens from red felt and 2 cuffs from black felt.
2. Place mitten shapes together. Thread black yarn onto needle. Leaving top edge open, work Overcast Stitch, page 159, around edges of mitten; knot and trim yarn ends.
3. Place cuff pieces on front and back at top of mitten; glue to secure. Using 2 strands of embroidery floss, work Overcast Stitch to join side edges of cuff pieces together.
4. For snowflake appliqué, trace snowflake B and C patterns, page 15, onto tracing paper; cut out. Use small scissors to cut snowflake B from black felt and snowflake C from ivory felt. Layer and glue shapes together. Glue button to center of snowflake.
5. Glue snowflake to mitten.
6. For hanger, fold red yarn length into a loop and glue ends to inside top at thumb side of mitten.

SNOWFLAKE A

MITTEN
(cut 2)

CUFF
(cut 2)

BELLPULLS (Shown on page 10)

For each bellpull, you will need a 7" x 11" piece of oatmeal Rustico® evenweave fabric (14 ct), red embroidery floss (see color key), embroidery hoop (optional), an approx. 6½" long twig, 12" of ¼"w red grosgrain ribbon, silver jingle bell, removable fabric marking pen, and fabric glue.

1. Follow **Cross Stitch** instructions, page 158, to stitch design at center of fabric, extending border 2" beyond top of design. Use 3 strands of floss for Cross Stitch.
2. Use pen to lightly draw lines on fabric ½" from top and 1½" from sides and bottom of stitched design. Cut out stitched piece along drawn lines.
3. Leaving a ⅜" border around stitched design, press side and bottom edges of stitched piece to back and glue in place.
4. Use floss to sew bell to point of ornament.
5. For hanger casing, press top of ornament 1½" to back. Glue edge in place. Insert twig in casing. Knot 1 end of ribbon around each end of twig.

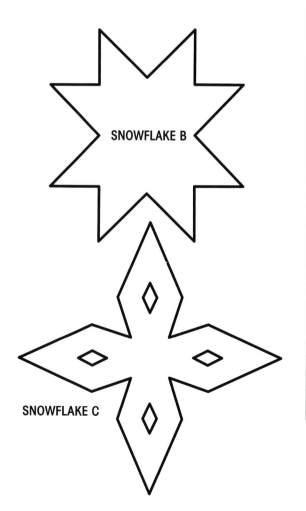

SNOWFLAKE B

SNOWFLAKE C

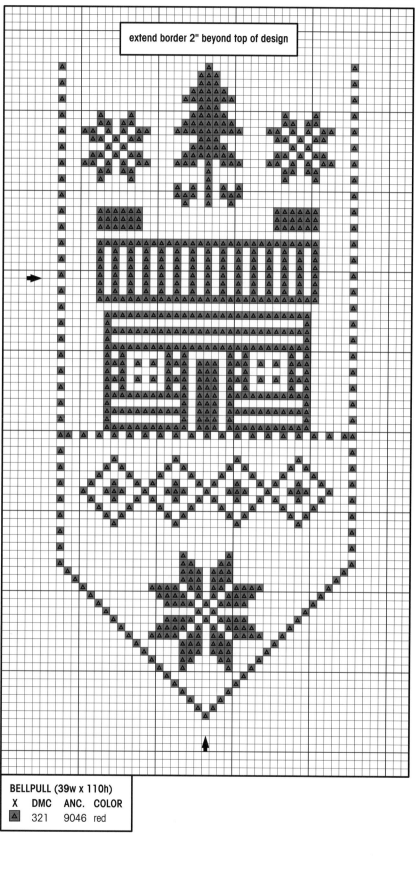

extend border 2" beyond top of design

BELLPULL (39w x 110h)			
X	DMC	ANC.	COLOR
▲	321	9046	red

15

SLED ORNAMENTS

(Shown on page 10)

For each ornament, you will need a 7" long mini wooden sled, red acrylic paint, flat paintbrush, brown felt-tip pen (if needed), tracing paper, graphite transfer paper, soft eraser (if needed), metal ruler, and a woodburning pen with universal and flow points (we used a Walnut Hollow Farm Creative Woodburner).

1. Use a pencil to draw lines about ¼" inside edges on top of sled for border.

2. (**Note:** For Step 2, follow **Woodburning** instructions, page 160.) Transfer small reindeer pattern to center top of sled. Burn lines on sled for border and outline of reindeer. Fill in reindeer.

3. Use red paint to paint border and sides of top of sled and rod at front of sled. If necessary, use pen to draw over burned lines of border.

SNAPSHOT ORNAMENTS

(Shown on page 10)

For each ornament, you will need a 4" square of ³/₃₂"- thick balsa wood, a 3½" square cut from a photocopy of a photograph, wood-tone spray, 5" of floral wire, a glue gun, and a woodburning pen with universal and flow points (we used a Walnut Hollow Farm Creative Woodburner).

1. Follow **Woodburning** instructions, page 160, to burn either a triangle border along edges of balsa wood square (holding woodburning pen with tip of point toward center of square) or other designs as desired.

2. Lightly spray photocopy with wood-tone spray.

3. Use small dots of glue to glue photocopy to center of balsa wood square.

4. For hanger, bend wire in half and glue ends to back of ornament.

NORDIC APPLIQUÉD TREE SKIRT (Shown on page 11)

For an approx. 56" dia. tree skirt, you will need one 56" square each of red felt for skirt top and ivory felt for underskirt; ivory, red, and black felt for appliqués; a 1"w x 2¼ yd bias strip of plaid flannel (pieced as necessary); 1"w fusible web tape; ivory thread; clear nylon thread; black yarn; large needle; assorted ½" dia. red and black buttons for appliqués; pinking shears; small sharp scissors; tracing paper; fabric marking pen; thumbtack or pin; string; and glue.

1. For underskirt, fold ivory felt square in half from top to bottom and again from left to right.

2. To mark outer cutting line, tie 1 end of string to fabric marking pen. Insert thumbtack through string 28" from pen. Insert thumbtack in felt as shown in **Fig. 1** and mark ¼ of a circle. Repeat to mark inner cutting line, inserting thumbtack through string 3" from pen.

Fig. 1

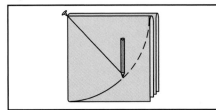

3. Cutting through each layer of felt, use pinking shears to cut out underskirt along marked lines.

4. For skirt top, use red felt square and repeat Steps 1 - 3, inserting thumbtack through string 27" from pen for outer cutting line and 3½" from pen for inner cutting line and using regular scissors to cut out shape.

5. Thread black yarn onto needle and work Overcast Stitch, page 159, along outer edge of skirt top.

6. Center skirt top over underskirt and pin in place.

7. For opening at back of skirt, use a yardstick and fabric marking pen to draw a line on skirt from inner to outer edge of layered shapes. Stitch layers together ¼" on each side of drawn line. Use pinking shears to cut through both layers along drawn line.

8. For plaid trim, fuse web tape to wrong side of bias flannel strip. Beginning at 1 opening edge, fuse strip about 2" from outer edge of skirt top. Use nylon thread and a medium width zigzag stitch with a short stitch length to stitch over long edges of strip.

9. (**Note:** Follow Step 9 to make 3 tree appliqués and 6 reindeer appliqués; turn traced pattern over before stitching to make 3 of the reindeer appliqués in reverse.) Use tree pattern, page 18, and large reindeer pattern, this page, and follow Cutwork Snowflakes instructions, page 14, to make appliqués, using one 7" square each of tracing paper, red felt, and ivory felt for each tree appliqué and one 9" square each of tracing paper, red felt, and ivory felt for each reindeer appliqué.

10. (**Note:** Follow Step 10 to make 7 snowflake appliqués.) For each snowflake appliqué, follow Step 4 of Mitten Ornaments instructions, page 14. Glue snowflake appliqué to a piece of red felt. Cutting close to snowflake, cut snowflake from red felt.

11. Arrange appliqués on tree skirt; glue to secure.

RUSTIC THROW PILLOW (Shown on page 12)

For a 17" x 12" pillow, you will need two 13" x 18" pieces of flannel for pillow front and back; ivory, red, and black felt for pillow flap and appliqués; polyester fiberfill; ivory thread and thread to match fabrics; black yarn; large needle; three ¹/₂" dia. black buttons; four ³/₄" dia. silver shank buttons; small sharp scissors; and fabric glue.

1. For pillow, place pillow front and back flannel pieces right sides together. Using a ¹/₂" seam allowance and leaving an opening for turning, sew front and back fabric pieces together. Clip corners, turn pillow right side out, and press. Stuff pillow with fiberfill. Sew final closure by hand.

2. For appliqués, use tree pattern, page 18, and snowflake D pattern and follow Cutwork Snowflakes instructions, page 14, using one 7" square each of tracing paper, red felt, and ivory felt for each appliqué.

3. Use dots of glue to glue each snowflake appliqué to a black felt piece. Cutting close to snowflake, cut snowflake from black felt.

4. Glue black buttons to appliqués.

5. For pillow flap, cut an 8" x 17¹/₄" piece of red felt. Thread a 2¹/₄ yd length of yarn onto needle and work Overcast Stitch, page 159, along side and bottom edges of felt piece. Knot and trim yarn ends.

6. Glue appliqués to flap.

7. Place top edge of flap along 1 long edge (top) of pillow. Spacing silver buttons evenly across top of flap, sew buttons and flap to pillow.

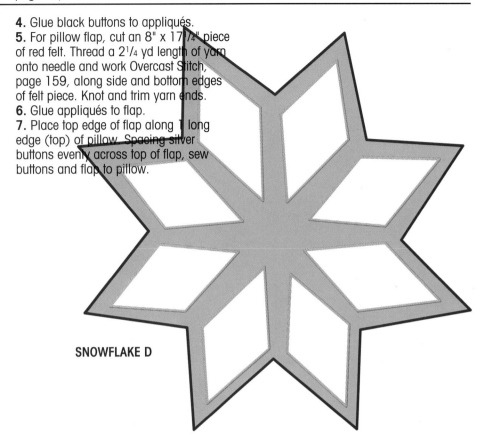

SNOWFLAKE D

COVERED LAMP (Shown on page 13)

You will need a lamp, self-adhesive lampshade, plaid flannel to cover lamp, red felt to cover shade, polyester fiberfill, ¹/₄" dia. jute rope, 2 approx. 1¹/₂" long pinecones, ¹/₄"w elastic, black yarn, large needle, fray preventative, glue gun, fabric marking pen, thumbtack or pin, string, and 1 Cutwork Snowflake (page 14).

1. To cover lamp base, refer to **Fig. 1** and measure lamp from 1 side of neck to opposite side of neck; add 14". Cut a square of flannel the determined measurement.

Fig. 1

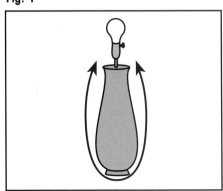

2. To cut circle from fabric square, fold square in half from top to bottom and again from left to right. Tie 1 end of string to fabric marking pen. Measure ¹/₂ the measurement determined in Step 1 from the pen; insert thumbtack through string at this point. Referring to **Fig. 1** of Nordic Appliquéd Tree Skirt, page 16, mark ¹/₄ of a circle on fabric. Cutting through all layers, cut fabric along drawn line.

3. Center lamp on wrong side of fabric circle. Mark fabric where lamp cord extends from base of lamp. Cut a small slit in fabric at mark large enough for plug at end of cord to fit through. Apply fray preventative to raw edges of slit. Pull cord through slit.

4. Bring edges of fabric up and gather around neck of lamp, placing fiberfill between lamp and fabric to achieve desired fullness. Knot elastic securely around fabric and neck of lamp (**Fig. 2**). Trim ends of elastic. Fold raw edges of fabric to wrong side and tuck under elastic.

Fig. 2

5. Wrap a 2 yd length of rope around neck of lamp, covering elastic; knot rope ends together at front of lamp. Knot each end of rope and glue 1 pinecone to each end.

6. For lampshade, follow manufacturer's instructions to cut shape to cover shade from red felt. Thread yarn onto needle and work Overcast Stitch, page 159, along long edge of felt shape; knot and trim ends. Cover shade with felt shape. Glue a length of rope along top edge of shade.

7. Glue snowflake to shade. Place shade on lamp.

NORDIC APPLIQUÉD STOCKINGS (Shown on page 11)

For each stocking, you will need ivory, red, and black felt; fusible knit interfacing; ivory thread and thread to match stocking fabric; assorted 1/2" dia. red and black buttons for appliqués; one 3/4" dia. silver shank button for cuff; small sharp scissors; pinking shears; tracing paper; and fabric glue.

For tree stocking, you will **also** need an 18" x 24" piece of red felt for stocking, a 15" x 18" piece of plaid flannel for cuff, black yarn, and a large needle.

For snowflake stocking, you will **also** need an 18" x 24" piece of plaid flannel for stocking and a fabric marking pen.

TREE STOCKING

1. For stocking pattern, match dotted lines and align arrows and trace top and bottom of stocking pattern onto tracing paper; cut out.

2. Use pattern to cut 2 stocking shapes from felt.

3. Pin stocking shapes together. Thread a 1 1/2 yd length of yarn onto needle. Leaving top edge open, work Overcast Stitch, page 159, along side and bottom edges of stocking; knot and trim yarn ends.

4. For hanger, use pinking shears to cut a 1" x 6" strip of black felt. Fold strip in half to form a loop. Matching ends of loop to top edge of stocking, pin loop inside stocking near heel-side seamline.

5. (**Note:** Use a 1/2" seam allowance for all sewing steps.) For cuff, fuse interfacing to wrong side of flannel. Measure around top of stocking; add 1". Cut a piece of flannel 13" wide by the determined measurement. Matching right sides and short edges, fold flannel piece in half. Sew short edges together to form a tube. Press seam allowance open. Matching wrong sides and raw edges, fold tube in half.

6. To attach cuff to stocking, place cuff in stocking, matching raw edges of cuff with top edge of stocking and seamline of cuff to heelside seamline of stocking. Sew cuff to stocking. Fold cuff down over stocking.

7. Sew silver button to top of cuff close to hanger.

8. For tree appliqué, use tree pattern and follow Cutwork Snowflakes instructions, page 14, using one 7" square each of tracing paper, red felt, and ivory felt. Glue a black button to appliqué. Glue appliqué to stocking.

9. For each snowflake appliqué, follow Step 4 of Mitten Ornaments instructions, page 14. Glue appliqués to stocking.

SNOWFLAKE STOCKING

1. For stocking pattern, follow Step 1 of Tree Stocking instructions.

2. Fuse interfacing to wrong side of stocking fabric piece.

3. Using stocking pattern and leaving top edge open, follow **Sewing Shapes**, page 158, to make stocking from fabric pieces.

4. For cuff, measure around top of stocking; add 1". Cut a piece of black felt 6 1/2" wide by the determined measurement.

5. For trim on cuff, use pinking shears to cut a strip of red felt 1/2" wide and same length as cuff felt piece. Glue strip along 1 long edge (bottom) of cuff felt piece.

6. (**Note:** Use a 1/2" seam allowance for remaining sewing steps.) Matching right sides and short edges, fold cuff piece in half. Sew short edges of cuff piece together to form a tube. Press seam allowance open and turn right side out.

7. To make hanger and attach hanger and cuff to stocking, follow Steps 4, 6, and 7 of Tree Stocking instructions.

8. For snowflake appliqué, use snowflake D pattern, page 17, and follow Cutwork Snowflakes instructions, page 14, using one 7" square each of tracing paper, red felt, and ivory felt. Glue a black button to appliqué. Glue appliqué to cuff.

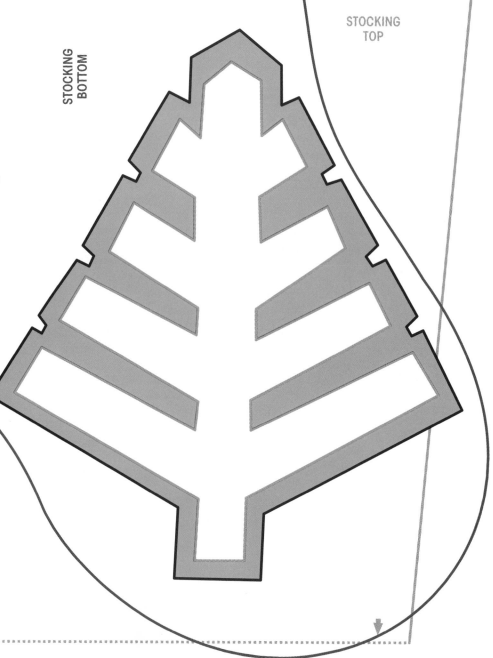

STOCKING
TOP

STOCKING
BOTTOM

ICE CANDLES
(Shown on page 12)

For each candle, you will need either Candle Magic® Wax Crystals or paraffin (we used about 4.5 ounces of crystals for small candle and 9 ounces of crystals for large candle); Candle Magic® Wax Stick-ums; an empty milk carton (we used a ¹/₂-pint carton for small candle and a 1-pint carton for large candle); a taper or votive candle same color as wax; miniature pinecones, pepperberries, and preserved cedar and pine to decorate candle; utility knife; newspaper; hand-held hair dryer (if needed); ice; coffee can for melting wax; and a pan to hold can.

Caution: Do not melt wax over an open flame or directly on burner. Do not leave burning candles unattended.

1. Rinse and dry carton. Use utility knife to cut away top of carton.
2. Place candle in center of carton. If necessary, use knife to trim bottom of candle so top of candle is just below top of carton. Use Wax Stick-ums to secure candle in carton.
3. Reserving some decorations, use Wax Stick-ums to secure pinecones, pepperberries, and greenery to inside walls of carton, pressing greenery flat against walls.
4. Cover work area with newspaper. Place wax crystals in can. Place can in pan and fill pan half full with water. Heat water until wax crystals melt.
5. Crack ice into small pieces (size of ice will determine size of holes in candle). Arrange ice around candle in carton. Before ice melts, pour melted wax into carton in a continuous stream until wax is level with top of candle; do not cover wick. (Wax fills open spaces between ice pieces and melts ice, forming holes in candle.)
6. Before wax hardens, place reserved decorations into wax at top of candle, keeping decorations close to sides of candle and away from candle wick.
7. After wax has hardened, pour water from carton and carefully peel carton from candle.
8. If necessary, use hair dryer to melt thin layers of wax covering decorations, open holes, and smooth rough edges on outside of candle. Use fingernail to scrape Wax Stick-ums residue from candle.

WINTRY WOODBURNED FRAMES (Shown on page 13)

For each frame, you will need a photocopy of a photograph to fit in frame, wood-tone spray, lightweight cardboard, tracing paper, glue gun, and a woodburning pen with universal point (we used a Walnut Hollow Farm Creative Woodburner).
For snowflake frame, you will **also** need a large wooden frame (our frame measures 8¹/₄" x 10¹/₄" and holds a 5" x 7" picture), flow point for woodburning pen, ribbon about same width as side of frame for trim, graphite transfer paper, soft eraser (if needed), and a metal ruler.
For twig frame, you will **also** need a small wooden frame (our frame measures 6¹/₄" x 5¹/₄" and holds a 4" x 6" picture); twigs to cover frame; ivory, red, and black felt; ¹/₂" dia. red button; small sharp scissors; and a utility knife.

SNOWFLAKE FRAME
1. (**Note:** For Step 1, follow **Woodburning** instructions, page 160.) Transfer snowflake patterns to frame. Burn lines and dots of snowflakes. For border along frame opening, burn 3 lines at each corner of frame opening. Burn straight lines about ¹/₄" apart along inside edge of frame opening. For triangle border, hold pen with tip pointing toward outer edge of frame and burn triangles along opening of frame. Burn small dots as desired along triangle border.
2. For trim, measure around outer edges of frame; add 1". Cut a length of ribbon the determined measurement; press 1 end ¹/₂" to wrong side. Starting at center bottom of frame and overlapping pressed end over raw end, glue ribbon to sides of frame.
3. For photograph and backing, cut a piece of cardboard to fit in frame. Lightly spray photocopy of photograph with wood-tone spray. Glue photocopy to cardboard. Insert in frame and glue to secure.

TWIG FRAME
1. Use utility knife to cut twigs to fit on front of frame (we used 10 approx. 6¹/₄" long twigs for sides and 9 approx. 3" long twigs for top and bottom).
2. Glue twigs to frame.
3. Follow **Woodburning** instructions, page 160, and use universal point to burn short straight lines along twigs on frame.
4. For photograph and backing, follow Step 3 of Snowflake Frame instructions.
5. For snowflake appliqué, follow Step 4 of Mitten Ornaments instructions, page 14. Glue snowflake to a piece of red felt. Cutting close to snowflake, cut snowflake from red felt. Glue snowflake to frame.

SNOWFLAKES

SANTA'S SWEETSHOP

Designed to delight people of all ages, our Santa's Sweetshop collection is laden with scrumptious make-believe cookies, cakes, and confections! The sweet tree embellishments include everything from gingerbread men to cleverly constructed lollipops. There are even garlands of goodies playfully strung among the frosty white branches. For a yummy finish, a cheery skirt trimmed with giant "gumdrops" encircles the base of the tree. Youngsters will love the peppermint Advent calendar and candy ball sun catchers, too. Instructions for the projects shown here and on the following pages begin on page 24.

Featuring a cute gingerbread man and lollipop accents, our no-sew **Peppermint Advent Calendar** *(page 27)* is a fun way for children to count down the days until Christmas. Numbered peppermints are simply taped to the wall hanging for easy removal.

Adorned with tantalizing treats, our **Santa's Sweetshop Tree** *(page 24)* is a dreamy sight! Tucked among the branches are **Chocolate Loaf Cakes** *(page 24)* and **Ice-Cream Cones** *(page 27)*, which look good enough to eat. Precious **Gingerbread Men** *(page 24)* fashioned from foam core board are covered with brown tissue paper and dressed up with various trims. Miniature **Cookie Sheets** *(page 24)* feature small gingerbread cookies "iced" with dimensional paint, and **Playful Lollipops** *(page 24)* glisten with "sugary" spirals. Embellished with fabric circles and hand-colored signs, **Sweetshop Tart Pans** *(page 27)* make nifty ornaments, too! Wispy wired-ribbon bows and a garland of colorful cereal and star-shaped marshmallows complete the imaginative tree.

Clear plastic ball ornaments are filled with a variety of candies for these delightful window decorations. Completed with pretty polka-dot bows and ribbon hangers, the terrific treats can also be given as favors.

Our **Goody Gumdrop Tree Skirt** (*page 26*) is a wonderful complement to the tree. Colorful gumdrop-shaped cutouts and jumbo white rickrack "icing" are glued along the edges of a large fabric circle.

SANTA'S SWEETSHOP TREE
(Shown on page 21)

This winter wonderland of a tree will fulfill the wishes of children of all ages this Christmas season. Real and faux treats combine on the 7-foot-tall flocked tree, which is filled with delicious, delightful goodies straight from Santa's special sweetshop.

Decorations begin with three "tree-riffic" garlands—sugary cereal pieces and marshmallow shapes are strung on cotton string for one of the garlands, the caramel corn garland is an artificial popcorn garland spritzed with wood-tone spray, and a purchased purple foil ribbon garland playfully winds among the boughs. Sheer yellow bows add pretty dashes of sunshine to the frosted tree.

Bakery and ice-cream sweets inspire simple ornaments that look good enough to eat. Our Gingerbread Men (this page) are tissue paper-covered foam core board cutouts. Little oven-fresh gingerbread boys on Cookie Sheets (this page) are purchased cookies iced with white dimensional paint. Other bakery delights include mini Chocolate Loaf Cakes (this page) and Sweetshop Tart Pans (page 27). Playful Lollipops (this page) add spirals of sweet colors, and the Ice-cream Cones (page 27) are single and double scoops of melt-free goodness with a dollop of "whipped cream" and an artificial cherry on top.

Our Goody Gumdrop Tree Skirt (page 26) completes this pretty, pastel tree. Fused gumdrop fabric shapes along the edge of the skirt make it a cute no-sew tree accent.

COOKIE SHEETS
(Shown on page 22)

For each cookie sheet, you will need a 5" x 7" piece of craft metal (we used Homestead Metal Craft by Toolin' Station), 9 approx. 2"h gingerbread man cookies without icing, white dimensional paint, polyurethane varnish, foam brush, tin snips, floral wire, wire cutters, and household cement.

1. For cookie sheet, use tin snips to round corners at 1 end of metal piece. Bend about $1/2$" of rounded end up.
2. Use foam brush to apply varnish to cookies. Use paint to "ice" cookies.
3. Glue cookies to cookie sheet.
4. For hanger, glue center of a length of wire to back of cookie sheet.

CHOCOLATE LOAF CAKES
(Shown on page 22)

For each cake, you will need a mini loaf pan (ours are $4^1/4$" x $2^1/4$" x $1^1/4$"), floral foam brick, dark brown acrylic spray paint, Liquitex® Titanium White Structural Paint™, iridescent glitter, assorted seed and bugle beads, a silk holly sprig with berries, a craft stick, floral wire, wire cutters, and a glue gun.

1. Cut a piece from foam brick to fit in pan and extend about $3/4$" above rim.
2. Spray paint foam piece brown.
3. Glue foam piece into pan.
4. Use craft stick to spread structural paint over top of foam piece. Before paint dries, cut leaves and berries from sprig and center on top of cake. Sprinkle cake with glitter and beads.
5. For hanger, glue center of a length of wire to bottom of pan.

PLAYFUL LOLLIPOPS
(Shown on page 22)

For each lollipop, you will need a 4" square of pink or yellow satin, fusible web, 15" of $1^1/2$"w wired polka-dot satin ribbon, $3/4$ yd of $1/4$" dia. cotton cord, purple acrylic paint, paintbrushes, poster board, a jumbo craft stick, utility scissors, iridescent glitter, 8" of clear nylon thread, craft glue, and a glue gun.

1. Fuse satin to poster board. Cut a 3" dia. circle from fabric-covered poster board.
2. Wind cord into a spiral on satin side of circle; use craft glue to secure.
3. Thin craft glue with water. Use a paintbrush to lightly coat cord with glue; sprinkle with glitter. When glue is dry, shake to remove excess glitter.
4. For stick, use scissors to cut 1 round end from craft stick. Paint stick purple. With cord end at bottom of circle, hot glue remaining round end of stick to center back of circle.
5. Tie ribbon into a bow and hot glue to lollipop, covering end of cord.
6. For hanger, knot ends of nylon thread; hot glue knot to top back of lollipop.

GINGERBREAD MEN
(Shown on page 22)

For each gingerbread man, you will need foam core board; fabric for vest; 8" of $5/8$"w grosgrain ribbon; two $1/2$" dia. white buttons; white, pink, and black dimensional paint; wood-tone spray; tan tissue paper; floral wire; wire cutters; utility knife; spray adhesive; and a glue gun.

1. Trace gingerbread man and vest patterns separately onto tracing paper; cut out.
2. Lightly spray tissue paper with wood tone spray.
3. Lightly draw around gingerbread man pattern once on foam core board and twice on tissue paper. Use utility knife to cut shape from foam core board. Cut out 1 tissue paper shape about $1/2$" outside drawn lines and remaining shape along drawn lines.
4. Apply spray adhesive to front and edges of foam core board shape. Center large tissue paper shape on foam core board shape and press in place; wrap edges of paper to back of foam core board, clipping edges of paper and applying additional adhesive and small paper scraps to edges of shape as necessary to cover edges. Apply spray adhesive to back of foam core board shape. Press remaining tissue paper shape in place on back of foam core board shape.
5. Use vest pattern to cut vest from fabric. Use spray adhesive to glue vest to gingerbread man. Tie ribbon length into a bow; hot glue bow and buttons to vest.
6. Paint black mouth and eyes, pink cheeks, and white icing on gingerbread man.
7. For hanger, hot glue center of a length of wire to back of gingerbread man.

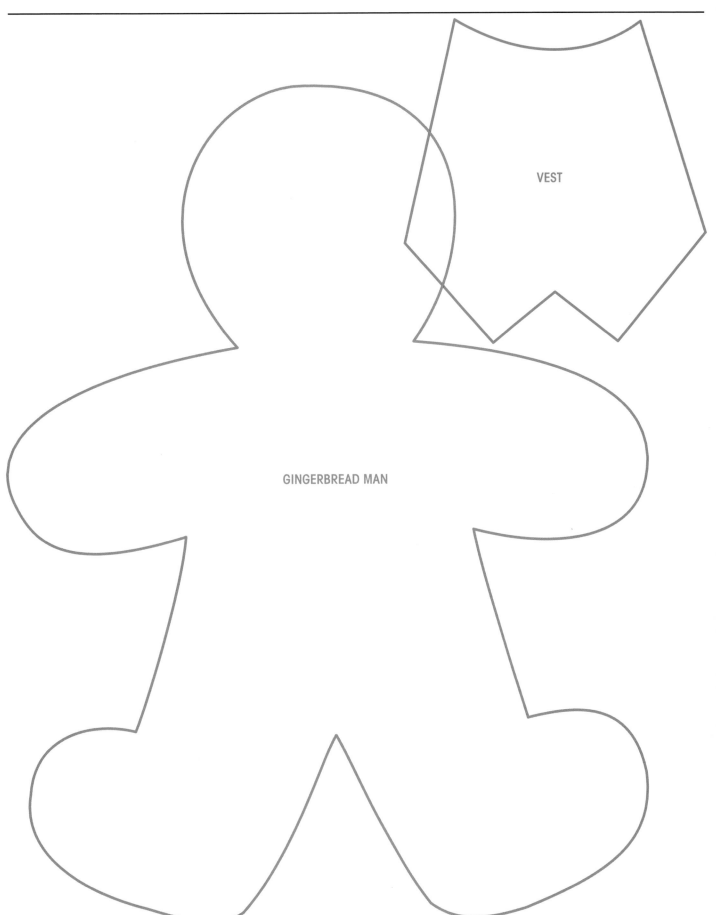

VEST

GINGERBREAD MAN

GOODY GUMDROP TREE SKIRT (Shown on page 23)

For an approx. 52" dia. tree skirt, you will need a 45" fabric square, assorted fabrics for gumdrop border, 1/2"w fusible web tape, fusible web, heavy fusible interfacing, jumbo rickrack, tracing paper, fabric marking pen, thumbtack or pin, string, and fabric glue.

1. For skirt, fold fabric square in half from top to bottom and again from left to right.
2. To mark outer cutting line, tie 1 end of string to fabric marking pen. Insert thumbtack through string 22" from pen. Insert thumbtack in fabric as shown in **Fig. 1** and mark 1/4 of a circle. Repeat to mark inner cutting line, inserting thumbtack through string 1 1/2" from pen.

Fig. 1

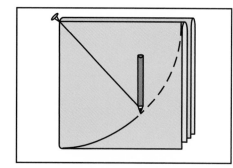

3. Cutting through all layers of fabric, cut out skirt along marked lines. For opening at back of skirt, cut along 1 fold from inner to outer edge.
4. To hem inner and opening edges of skirt, fuse web tape to wrong side of fabric along each edge. Make 1/2" clips about 1/2" apart along inner edge. Fold inner and opening edges 1/2" to wrong side and fuse in place.

5. For gumdrop border, trace pattern onto tracing paper; cut out. Use pattern to cut 19 gumdrop shapes from interfacing. For each gumdrop, fuse web to wrong side of fabric. Carefully fuse interfacing shape to wrong side of fabric. Cutting about 1/2" from side and bottom edges and even with top edge of shape, cut shape from fabric. Make clips at about 1" intervals in side and bottom edges of fabric shape to about 1/8" from interfacing. Fold clipped edges to back over interfacing shape and fuse in place.
6. Overlapping tops of gumdrops about 1/2" onto skirt, arrange and glue gumdrops along edge on right side of skirt.
7. For trim, glue rickrack along skirt edge over raw edges of gumdrops, gluing 1/2" of trim to back of skirt at each opening edge.

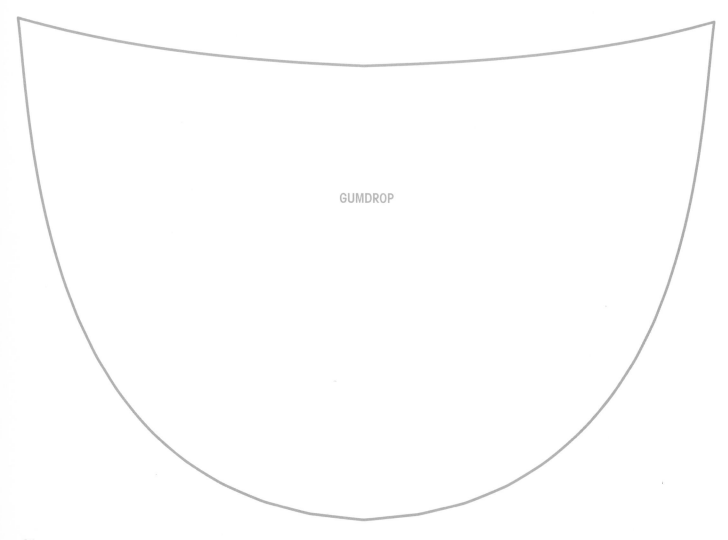

GUMDROP

ICE-CREAM CONES
(Shown on page 22)

For each ice-cream cone, you will need one 2¹/₂" dia. plastic foam ball for each ice-cream dip, a sugar cone, Liquitex® Titanium White Structural Paint™, acrylic paint (we used pink and green), polyurethane varnish, foam brush, palette knife or craft stick, assorted seed and bugle beads, artificial cherry, clear nylon thread for hanger, utility knife (if needed), and a glue gun.

1. Use foam brush to apply varnish to sugar cone.
2. Glue 1 foam ball into top of cone. For a double-dip cone, use utility knife to flatten bottom of second foam ball. Glue bottom of ball to top of ball in cone.
3. Use acrylic paint to tint structural paint desired color(s). Use palette knife to apply structural paint to foam ball(s).
4. For whipped cream, apply a dollop of white structural paint to top of ice-cream cone. Press cherry into paint. Before paint dries, sprinkle with beads.
5. For hanger, knot ends of a 12" length of nylon thread; glue knot to top of ornament.

SWEETSHOP TART PANS (Shown on page 22)

For each tart pan, you will need a 4" dia. tart pan, a 4" dia. pinked fabric circle, white paper, colored pencils, black pen, floral wire, wire cutters, and a glue gun.

1. Trace pattern onto white paper.
2. Color design with colored pencils. Use black pen to draw over lines and dots of design. Cut out design.

3. Glue fabric circle and paper circle into bottom of pan.
4. For hanger, glue center of a length of wire to bottom of pan.

PEPPERMINT ADVENT CALENDAR (Shown on page 20)

For a 21¹/₂" x 25" calendar, you will need fabric for calendar and hanging loops; fabrics for border and to cover rod; fusible web; ³/₄"w fusible web tape; fusible interfacing; 6 assorted ⁵/₈" dia. buttons; 1¹/₂ yds of ⁵/₈"w grosgrain ribbon; 19¹/₂" of jumbo rickrack; 24 wrapped peppermint candies; black permanent felt-tip pen; 22¹/₂" of ⁷/₈" dia. dowel rod; two 1" dia. wooden finials; acrylic paint and paintbrush for finials; double-stick tape; a glue gun; the following items for lollipops: one 4" square each of yellow and pink satin, two ³/₄ yd lengths of ¹/₄" dia. cotton cord, 15" each of two different 1¹/₂"w satin ribbons, 2 wrapped candy sticks, paintbrush, iridescent glitter, poster board, and craft glue; and 1 Gingerbread Man (page 24) without hanger.

1. Cut a 23" x 26¹/₂" piece of fabric and a 21¹/₂" x 25" piece of interfacing for calendar. Center and fuse interfacing to

wrong side of fabric piece. Fuse web tape along each edge on wrong side of fabric piece. Press edges to wrong side over interfacing and fuse in place.
2. For border, fuse web to wrong sides of fabrics. Cut 1¹/₈"w strips of various lengths from fabrics. Overlapping ends, fuse strips about 1" from edges of calendar.
3. (**Note:** Use hot glue unless otherwise indicated.) Center and glue rickrack to calendar about 12" from top.
4. Glue Gingerbread Man to calendar.
5. For lollipops, follow Steps 1 - 3 of Playful Lollipops instructions, page 24, to make top of each lollipop. Tie each 1¹/₂"w ribbon length into a bow; trim ends. Arrange tops of lollipops, candy sticks, and bows on calendar at each side of Gingerbread Man; glue in place.
6. Cut six 9" lengths from ⁵/₈"w ribbon. Spacing evenly, glue ribbon lengths to calendar. Glue 1 button to top of each ribbon length.

7. For hanging loops, cut four 2¹/₂" x 6" strips from fabric. Fuse web tape along center on wrong side of each fabric strip. Fuse long edges of each strip to center. Matching ends, fold strips in half to form loops. Spacing loops evenly, glue about 1" of ends of loops to top back of calendar.
8. For covered rod, cut a 3" x 24" fabric strip. Center and wrap fabric strip around dowel rod and glue to secure, overlapping long edges. Fold ends of fabric onto ends of rod and glue to secure. Paint finials and glue to ends of rod.
9. Insert rod through loops on calendar.
10. Use pen to write numbers on wrappers of candy pieces. Spacing evenly, use pieces of double-stick tape to tape candies to calendar.

SACRED CELEBRATION

*B*efitting the most sacred of celebrations, our Christmas collection
features glorious decorations fashioned in rich jewel tones and enhanced with
golden flourishes. From the faux stained-glass scene depicting Madonna and Child
to the elegant mosaic trinket boxes, each project reflects the refined artistry found
in European cathedrals. This Olde-World influence is also evident in the exquisite
trims for the evergreen. A tapestry photo album and coordinating gift wrap
complete this divine treasury. Instructions for the projects shown
here and on the following pages begin on page 34.

Portraying a tender Yuletide scene, our **Madonna and Child Triptych** *(page 38)* is a beautiful display for an end table,
mantel, or shelf. The stained-glass effect is created using colored tissue paper, glue, and dimensional paint. Tassels and
gemstone accents add the finishing touch.

Our **Sacred Celebration Tree** *(page 34)* is a radiant vision adorned with **Regal Glass Ball Ornaments** *(page 37)* featuring jewels and luxurious trims, faux stained-glass **Madonna and Child Ornaments** *(page 34)*, and **Mosaic Balls** *(page 36)* covered with gilded paper cutouts. Red iridescent bows and **Oval Star Mosaics** *(page 35)* continue the stately theme of the evergreen.

30

Symbolizing the Star of
Bethlehem that shone so
brilliantly on that holy
night, a **Sacred Star Tree
Topper** *(page 36)* appropriately
crowns our majestic evergreen.
The decoration is fashioned
using both the faux stained-
glass and mosaic techniques.

Perfect for holding small
treasures, our **Mosaic Trinket
Boxes** *(page 37)* make elegant
gift containers, as well as
beautiful tabletop accents.

To transform a plain album into this heirloom **Tapestry Photo Album** *(page 37)*, simply use batting, fabrics, trims, and an ornament from the tree. What a wonderful way to keep all your cherished Christmas memories in one place!

For exquisite presentations, try our **Star Gift Wrap and Tag** *(page 38)* and **Sponge-Painted Gift Wrap** *(page 34)*. Brown paper and wrapping paper are easily embellished with gold, turquoise, and red paint. Lush bows and other baubles complete the packages. To create several coordinating gift bags, simply apply the same techniques to purchased sacks.

A study in colorful contrasts, our **Mosaic Balls** (*page 36*) make a quick yet sophisticated display when simply arranged in a crystal bowl. The textured spheres are given an antique look with gold foil and black paint.

SACRED CELEBRATION TREE
(Shown on page 29)

To express the grandeur and hope of the Christmas season, we dressed this 7½-foot-tall tree with radiant stained-glass representations of Mary and Baby Jesus and gilded bejeweled ornaments, then crowned the tree with an elegant mosaic star.

The classic bead garlands, lustrous gold ropes accented with red stones, and distinctive chain garland with small ornaments add to the splendor of the tree as they wind among the boughs. The unique spindle ornaments are simple to make by spraying purchased ornaments with gold paint and gluing on gold trims. Luxuriant sheer red ribbon bows with golden edges are tied to the tips of the branches.

Ornaments to make include the Madonna and Child Ornaments (this page), which are gracious tributes to the holy season and are easily made by gluing pieces of colored tissue paper to plastic. The Regal Glass Ball Ornaments (page 37) include large glass balls embellished with paint and lavish trims and smaller ornaments trimmed to resemble glorious tassels. Cardboard ovals and plastic foam balls are covered with small pieces of painted illustration board and spackling to form the Oval Star Mosaics and Mosaic Balls (pages 35 and 36).

Atop the tree is the majestic Sacred Star Tree Topper (page 36), which is made using both the stained-glass and mosaic techniques from the ornaments.

To complete the splendid tree, a piece of tapestry fabric echoing the colors of the ornaments enfolds the base.

SPONGE-PAINTED GIFT WRAP
(Shown on page 32)

You will need brown kraft paper; metallic gold, antique gold, and dark red acrylic paint; sponge pieces; and paper towels.

Follow **Painting Techniques**, page 159, to sponge paint paper with dark red, antique gold, and gold paint.

MADONNA AND CHILD ORNAMENTS (Shown on page 30)

For each ornament, you will need a 6" x 8" piece of Aleene's Clear Shrink-It™ Plastic; ³/₄ yd of ³/₁₆"w gold cord; iridescent black dimensional paint; gold rub-on metallic finish; cream, dark red, purple, light turquoise, and turquoise tissue paper; paintbrushes; decoupage glue; permanent pen; and a low-temperature glue gun.

1. Use pen to trace outlines of ornament pattern onto plastic piece.
2. Use dimensional paint to paint over grey lines of pattern on plastic.
3. Follow Steps 5 and 6 of Madonna and Child Triptych, page 38, to color plastic.
4. Cut out design along outer lines.
5. Beginning at top point of ornament, hot glue cord along edges on front of ornament, looping cord at top to form hanger.

MADONNA AND CHILD ORNAMENT

OVAL STAR MOSAICS (Shown on page 30)

For each mosaic, you will need a 6" x 8" piece of mat board for ornament base; cold-press illustration board for mosaic pieces (available at art supply and craft stores); ⅝ yd of gold cord or trim; a 9mm gold bead; metallic gold, metallic copper, light red, dark red, light turquoise, turquoise, and black acrylic paint; paintbrushes; sponge pieces; gold craft foil and craft foil adhesive (we used Anita's Foil Leafing); spackling compound; glossy acrylic spray sealer; 4" of floral wire; rotary cutter or craft knife, cutting mat, and ruler (optional); tracing paper; graphite transfer paper; craft glue; a low-temperature glue gun; and newspaper.

1. For ornament base, trace pattern onto tracing paper. Use transfer paper to transfer pattern to mat board. Cut out shape along outer lines.

2. (**Note:** Cover work surface with newspaper. Refer to **Painting Techniques**, page 159, for sponge painting instructions.) For mosaic pieces, cut four 6" squares of illustration board. Paint 1 square each with the following colors: dark red sponge painted with light red, turquoise sponge painted with light turquoise, black sponge painted with metallic gold, and black sponge painted with metallic copper.

3. Cut out individual points of star pattern. Use patterns to cut points from red and turquoise illustration board.

4. Using transferred pattern as a guide, glue points to mat board oval.

5. (**Note:** When cutting remaining mosaic pieces, you can use either scissors, rotary cutter, or craft knife. To give your design a handmade look, cut pieces in varying shapes and sizes. When gluing pieces to oval, leave about ¹/₁₆" between pieces and between pieces and edge of mat board.) For remaining mosaic pieces, cut metallic gold and copper illustration board into approx. ⅝"w strips. Cut strips into irregularly shaped triangle and rectangle pieces to fit around star design on oval. Arrange pieces around star design and use craft glue to glue in place. Allow to dry 6 to 8 hours or overnight.

6. Mix black paint with a small amount of spackling until spackling is very dark grey (we used about ¹/₄ teaspoon paint for every tablespoon of spackling). For easier application, allow spackling to stand about 30 minutes before applying to mosaic design. Use fingers to apply spackling to mosaic design, pressing spackling between mosaic pieces. When spaces are filled, rub fingers over surface of design to remove excess spackling. Use a lightly dampened sponge piece to gently clean spackling residue from mosaic pieces. Allow spackling to dry.

Apply additional coats of spackling to design as needed to build spackling up to about the same level as mosaic pieces (we used 3 coats).

7. For highlights, follow manufacturer's instructions to apply gold foil to some of the gold mosaic pieces.

8. Allowing to dry between coats, apply several coats of sealer to ornament.

9. Hot glue gold bead to center of star and cord or trim along edges of ornament.

10. For hanger, fold wire in half to make a loop; hot glue ends of loop to top back of ornament.

OVAL STAR MOSAIC

SACRED STAR TREE TOPPER (Shown on page 31)

You will need a 9" x 12" piece of Aleene's Clear Shrink-It™ Plastic; ⁷⁄₈ yd of 1"w gold trim; iridescent black dimensional paint; gold rub-on metallic finish; dark red, purple, light turquoise, and turquoise tissue paper; paintbrushes; decoupage glue; permanent pen; a low-temperature glue gun; 10" of floral wire; and 1 Oval Star Mosaic (page 35).

1. Use pen to trace outlines of tree topper border pattern onto plastic piece.
2. Use dimensional paint to paint over grey lines of pattern on plastic.
3. Follow Steps 5 and 6 of Madonna and Child Triptych, page 38, to color plastic.
4. Cut out design along outer oval.
5. Hot glue Oval Star Mosaic to center front of plastic piece; glue trim along edges.
6. For hanger, hot glue center of wire to back of tree topper.

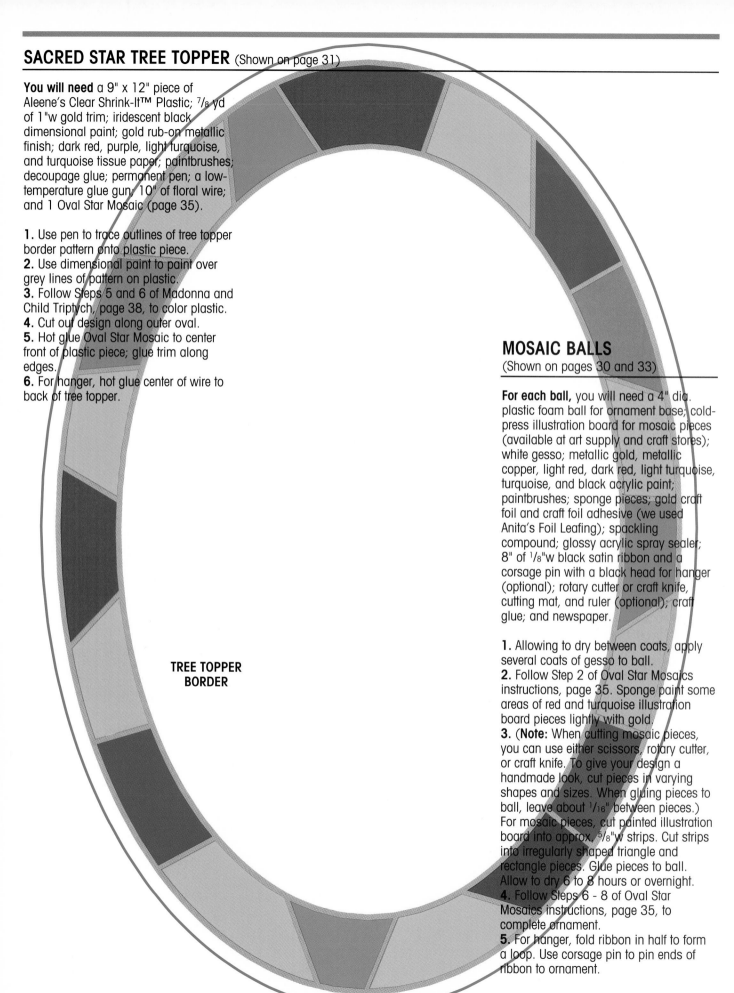

**TREE TOPPER
BORDER**

MOSAIC BALLS
(Shown on pages 30 and 33)

For each ball, you will need a 4" dia. plastic foam ball for ornament base; cold-press illustration board for mosaic pieces (available at art supply and craft stores); white gesso; metallic gold, metallic copper, light red, dark red, light turquoise, turquoise, and black acrylic paint; paintbrushes; sponge pieces; gold craft foil and craft foil adhesive (we used Anita's Foil Leafing); spackling compound; glossy acrylic spray sealer; 8" of ¹⁄₈"w black satin ribbon and a corsage pin with a black head for hanger (optional); rotary cutter or craft knife, cutting mat, and ruler (optional); craft glue; and newspaper.

1. Allowing to dry between coats, apply several coats of gesso to ball.
2. Follow Step 2 of Oval Star Mosaics instructions, page 35. Sponge paint some areas of red and turquoise illustration board pieces lightly with gold.
3. (**Note:** When cutting mosaic pieces, you can use either scissors, rotary cutter, or craft knife. To give your design a handmade look, cut pieces in varying shapes and sizes. When gluing pieces to ball, leave about ¹⁄₁₆" between pieces.) For mosaic pieces, cut painted illustration board into approx. ⁵⁄₈"w strips. Cut strips into irregularly shaped triangle and rectangle pieces. Glue pieces to ball. Allow to dry 6 to 8 hours or overnight.
4. Follow Steps 6 - 8 of Oval Star Mosaics instructions, page 35, to complete ornament.
5. For hanger, fold ribbon in half to form a loop. Use corsage pin to pin ends of ribbon to ornament.

REGAL GLASS BALL ORNAMENTS (Shown on page 30)

For each large ball ornament, you will need a 3" dia. glass ball ornament, assorted lace trims, a 2" long gold tassel, metallic gold spray paint, paper towels, and 8" of $3/8$"w sheer gold ribbon for hanger.

For each small ball ornament, you will need a $1 1/2$" to 2" dia. glass ball ornament, an 8" square of gold netting (if desired), about 7" of 6" long gold bullion fringe, 15" of $1 1/2$"w sheer gold ribbon, $3/8$ yd of $5/8$"w desired color sheer ribbon, large gold shank button, and 6" of $1/8$" dia. gold cord for hanger.

You will also need assorted gold trims, assorted acrylic jewels, and a glue gun.

LARGE BALL ORNAMENT

1. Glue lengths of lace and gold trims to ornament (we glued some trims around the ornaments and some from top to bottom). Cut hanger from tassel and glue tassel to bottom of ornament.
2. Glue jewels to ornament.

3. Spray paint ornament gold; before paint dries, use paper towel to remove some paint from jewels.
4. For hanger, thread ribbon through hanger on ornament; knot and trim ends.

SMALL BALL ORNAMENT

1. If desired, wrap ornament in netting square, gathering netting at top; glue to secure. Glue a length of gold trim around gathered netting at top of ornament and trim excess netting.
2. Glue lengths of gold trims to ornament (we glued some trims around the ornaments and some from top to bottom). Tightly roll bullion fringe and glue to secure. Glue fringe to bottom of ornament. Glue a length of trim around top of fringe.
3. Tie ribbons into bows; trim ends. Glue bows and button to top of ornament.
4. Glue jewels to ornament.
5. For hanger, thread cord through hanger on ornament; knot and fringe ends.

MOSAIC TRINKET BOXES (Shown on page 31)

For each box, you will need a papier-mâché box with lid (we used a $6 1/2$" oval box for star box, a $7 1/4$" square box, and a 4" dia. round box); cold-press illustration board for mosaic pieces (available at art supply and craft stores); assorted gold trims; metallic gold spray paint; metallic gold, metallic copper, light red, dark red, light turquoise, turquoise, and black acrylic paint; paintbrushes; sponge pieces; gold craft foil and craft foil adhesive (we used Anita's Foil Leafing); spackling compound; glossy acrylic spray sealer; rotary cutter or craft knife, cutting mat, and ruler (optional); craft glue; a low-temperature glue gun; and newspaper.

For star box, you will **also** need a 9mm gold bead, tracing paper, and graphite transfer paper.

For square box, you will **also** need gold ribbon and a gold drapery tieback with tassels.

STAR BOX

1. Spray paint box and sides of lid gold.
2. Trace oval star mosaic pattern, page 35, onto tracing paper. Use transfer paper to transfer star part of pattern to top of box lid. Treating top of lid as mat board oval, follow Steps 2 - 8 of Oval Star Mosaics instructions, page 35, to apply mosaic design to lid.

3. Hot glue gold bead to center of star on lid and trims to box as desired.

SQUARE BOX

1. Spray paint box and sides of lid gold.
2. Follow Step 2 of Oval Star Mosaics instructions, page 35. Sponge paint some areas of red and turquoise illustration board pieces lightly with gold.
3. (**Note:** When cutting mosaic pieces, you can use either scissors, rotary cutter, or craft knife. To give your design a handmade look, cut pieces in varying shapes and sizes. When gluing pieces to box lid, leave about $1/16$" between pieces and between pieces and edge of lid.) For mosaic pieces, cut painted illustration board into approx. $5/8$"w strips. Cut strips into irregularly shaped square and rectangle pieces. Glue pieces to top of box lid. Allow to dry 6 to 8 hours or overnight.
4. Follow Steps 6 - 8 of Oval Star Mosaics instructions, page 35, to complete box lid.
5. Glue gold trims to box as desired.
6. Place lid on box. Tie ribbon into a bow around box; trim ends. Tie cord with tassels into a bow around ribbon bow.

ROUND BOX

Follow Steps 1 - 5 of Square Box instructions.

TAPESTRY PHOTO ALBUM
(Shown on page 32)

You will need an approx. 10" x $11 1/2$" ring binder photo album, fabrics to cover album, a $6 1/2$" x $8 1/2$" piece of gold fabric, fusible web, polyester bonded batting, 1 yd of $1 1/2$"w gold ribbon, 32" each of 1"w and $5/8$"w gold trims, 4 large gold shank buttons, lightweight cardboard, a glue gun, and 1 Madonna and Child Ornament (page 34) without hanger.

1. To cover outside of album, measure width and height of open album. Cut a piece of batting the determined measurements. Cut a piece of fabric 2" larger on all sides than batting.
2. With album closed, glue batting to outside of album.
3. Center open album on wrong side of fabric piece. Glue corners of fabric diagonally over corners of album. Glue short edges of fabric over side edges of album. Glue long edges of fabric over top and bottom edges of album, trimming fabric to fit under album hardware.
4. For ribbon ties, cut ribbon in half. Glue 2" of 1 ribbon length to inside of album front at center of opening edge. Glue remaining ribbon length inside back of album. Trim ends of ties.
5. To cover inside of album, cut two 2"w fabric strips same length as height of album. Press ends of each strip $1/4$" to wrong side. Center and glue 1 strip along each side of album hardware with 1 long edge of each strip tucked under album hardware.
6. Cut 2 pieces of cardboard $1/4$" smaller on all sides than front of album. Cut 2 pieces of fabric 1" larger on all sides than 1 cardboard piece.
7. Center 1 cardboard piece on wrong side of 1 fabric piece. Glue corners of fabric diagonally over corners of cardboard. Glue edges of fabric over edges of cardboard. Repeat to cover remaining cardboard piece.
8. Center and glue covered cardboard pieces inside front and back of album.
9. For decoration on album, fuse web to wrong side of gold fabric piece. Center and fuse fabric piece to album front. Glue gold trims over edges of gold fabric piece and buttons to corners. Center and glue ornament to gold fabric piece.

STAR GIFT WRAP AND TAG
(Shown on page 32)

You will need dark red wrapping paper, metallic gold and turquoise acrylic paint, compressed craft sponge, small household paintbrush, tracing paper, permanent felt-tip pen, paper towels, and newspaper.

For tag, you will **also** need turquoise paper and craft glue.

GIFT WRAP

1. (**Note:** Cover work surface with newspaper.) For sponge shapes for sponge painting, trace star and gem patterns onto tracing paper; cut out. Use pen to draw around patterns on dry sponge. Cut out sponge shapes. Dampen shapes to expand.

2. To sponge paint designs on gift wrap, dip star sponge into gold paint; do not saturate. Blot on paper towel to remove excess paint. Using a stamping motion and reapplying paint to sponge as necessary, stamp stars on gift wrap as desired. Repeat to stamp gem design at center of each star.

3. To spatter paint gift wrap, dip paintbrush into diluted gold paint. Hold paintbrush over scrap paper and tap handle once to remove excess paint. Tap paintbrush over gift wrap. Repeat to spatter paint gift wrap with turquoise paint.

TAG

Cut star design from gift wrap and glue to paper. Cutting close to star, cut star from paper.

STAR

GEM

MADONNA AND CHILD TRIPTYCH (Shown on page 28)

You will need either a hinged triple frame with an 8" x 10" center frame and 3½" x 10" frames on each side (with glass included) or 3 individual frames and 4 small decorative brass hinges; a 3" x 9" piece of Aleene's Clear Shrink-It™ Plastic; six 25mm wooden beads; 2¾ yds of ⅜"w gold trim; 1 yd of ⅛" dia. gold cord; two 2½" long gold tassels; six gold acrylic jewels; iridescent black dimensional paint; gold rub-on metallic finish; gold craft foil and craft foil adhesive (we used Anita's Foil Leafing); metallic gold spray paint; cream, dark red, purple, light turquoise, and turquoise tissue paper; paintbrushes; decoupage glue; permanent pen; and a low-temperature glue gun.

1. (**Note:** Use caution when handling glass.) Remove glass panels from frame(s).

2. (**Note:** If you have a triple frame, go to Step 3.) Use hinges to join frames together to make a triple frame.

3. For large stained-glass panel, center large glass panel over triptych pattern. Use pen to trace outlines of pattern onto glass. Use dimensional paint to paint over grey lines of pattern on glass.

4. For small stained-glass panels, draw around 1 glass panel on tracing paper. Use a ruler and pencil to draw straight lines within drawn shape to resemble a stained-glass pattern. Using drawn pattern, repeat Step 3 for each small glass panel.

5. [**Note:** All areas of stained-glass panels except gold areas are colored by decoupaging tissue paper pieces onto unpainted side (back) of glass. Since the dye used in tissue paper "bleeds" when wet, apply all pieces of 1 color of tissue paper before applying the next color. For a darker shade of a color, apply 2 layers of paper.] Place desired color tissue paper over pattern and use a pencil to trace each area of that color onto tissue paper. Cut out tissue paper shapes just outside drawn lines. Use paintbrush to apply a thin coat of decoupage glue to glass within the painted outlines of 1 area. Place tissue paper piece over glue. Use brush to apply a coat of glue over tissue paper, wrinkling paper slightly with brush. Repeat until all areas of 1 color are filled. Repeat for each remaining color of tissue paper.

6. For gold areas of glass panels, use a paintbrush and follow manufacturer's instructions to apply several coats of rub-on finish to each area on back of glass panel.

7. Follow manufacturer's instructions to apply craft foil to halos and some gold areas on front of each glass panel.

8. For stained-glass panel at top of center part of frame, use pen to trace outlines of top panel pattern onto plastic piece. Use dimensional paint to paint over grey lines of pattern on plastic. Follow Steps 5 and 6 to color plastic. Cut out design along outer lines.

9. (**Note:** Use hot glue for remaining steps.) Glue beads to bottom of frame for feet.

10. Spray paint frame gold.

11. Secure glass panels in frames. Center and glue bottom of remaining stained-glass panel to top back of center part of frame.

12. Glue lengths of gold trim to front of each part of frame. Cut hangers from tassels. Glue 1 tassel to each end of cord. Glue cord along top of frame. Glue jewels to corners of center part of frame and to top of each tassel.

TOP
PANEL

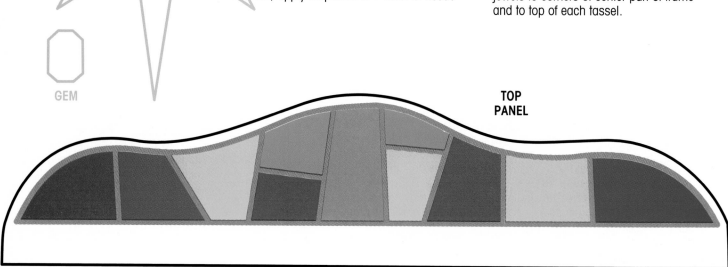

FOR SANTA COLLECTORS

Whether known as
Kris Kringle, Father Christmas,
St. Nick, or any number of
other names or faces, Santa's
essence remains the same —
that of a kindly gift-giver! Our
playful tree is decked with
several images of the North Pole
friend, as well as lists of good
little boys and girls, cute candy-
cane icicles, and miniature
reindeer feed bags. To continue
the holly-jolly theme, a framed
sign proclaims your affinity
for the fellow, boot-shaped
stockings are hung with cheer,
and a clever card holder is
fashioned from a window
shutter. You'll even discover
two festive shirts, along with a
gift bag for wrapping up small
tokens! Instructions for the
projects shown here and on
the following pages begin
on page 46.

(*Opposite*) From a star-waving Grandfather Frost to a sack-toting Santa Claus, our adorable **For Santa Collectors Tree** (*page 46*) features six **Painted Santas** (*page 46*) crafted from primed canvas. (Kris Kringle is shown on this page at bottom right.) Other trims for the evergreen include **Santa's List Ornaments** (*page 50*) topped with fabric holly leaves and peppermint "berries," red and white fabric **Reindeer Feed Bags** (*page 50*), candy-cane icicles, and wired-ribbon bows.

A nifty way to display holiday greetings, our **Shutter Card Holder** (*page 53*) is trimmed with fabric strips and oversize buttons. Two Santa ornaments add a coordinating touch to the Christmas accent.

For a sweet presentation, give your tokens tucked inside a **Jolly Gift Bag** (*page 53*). We used the St. Nicholas ornament for the tag, but you can use any of the Santa tree-trimmers, such as the joyful Kris Kringle pictured here.

Plain shirts are easily dressed up for the holidays with sweet St. Nick motifs. The striped **Santa Claus T-shirt** *(page 53)* depicts the frenzied fellow after he's delivered his bag of toys. The pattern is simply transferred onto the shirt and painted. For the **Santa Collector Sweatshirt** *(page 52)*, we machine appliquéd letter cutouts to the front and added painted faces and scattered button accents. *(Opposite, top)* A merry mantel topper, our **Santa Collector Sign** *(page 52)* is easy to make using fabric letter cutouts and painted Santa faces. *(Opposite, bottom)* Ribbon "shoelaces" and fleece cuffs enhance our **Christmas Boots** *(page 51)*.

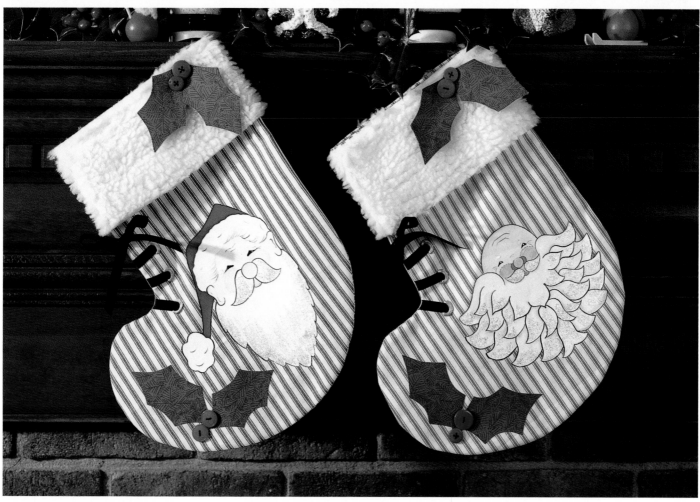

What could be better at Christmas than a tree decked with images of that lighthearted elf, Santa Claus? The collection on this happy 5-foot-tall tree includes six different Santa personalities, and we filled the tree with these twinkling good-humored gentlemen.

Red and white bead garlands are draped on the evergreen first, then shimmering green and red glass ball ornaments are added. Jaunty wired red ribbon bows are fastened to the tips of the branches.

Each of the Painted Santas (this page through page 50) has his own way of sharing the season. Old St. Nick has a fluffy beard, St. Nicholas has a white pom-pom glued to his starry hat, a smiling Father Christmas wears a red hat, a traditional Santa Claus carefully checks his list before stuffing his sack, Grandfather Frost flies among the branches spreading holiday cheer, and Kris Kringle holds a joyous message. Create a whimsical tree with all six or pick one or two to decorate your special tree.

Other ornaments on this merry tree include peppermint candy "icicles." To make the sweet ornaments, glue candy sticks to 1" dia. red glass ball ornaments and tie a tiny satin bow at the end of each one. Simple Reindeer Feed Bags (page 50) are made from cheery fabrics, and the Santa's List Ornaments (page 50) are made by gluing paper strips to fused fabric holly leaves.

To complete the tree, we wrapped the base with red and white checked fabric and added bright packages tied with oversize red bows.

PAINTED SANTAS (Shown on pages 42 and 43)

You will need primed artists' canvas; fusible web; acrylic paint (see color key on each page); iridescent glitter paint; paintbrushes; a palette; black permanent felt-tip pen; tracing paper; graphite transfer paper; paper towels; toothpicks; removable tape; a low-temperature glue gun; a 1/2" dia. wooden peg (Old St. Nick only); a 3/4" dia. white pom-pom (St. Nicholas only); two 1/2" dia. buttons (Father Christmas only); a 6"h plastic foam cone cut in half vertically (1 cone will make 2 ornaments), a 1 3/4"w wooden star cutout, a 3 1/2" long wooden craft pick, an 8mm red wooden bead for nose, and a utility knife (Grandfather Frost only); and black embroidery floss (Kris Kringle only).

OLD ST. NICK
1. Fuse wrong sides of two 7 1/2" canvas squares together.
2. Use pattern and follow **Painting Techniques**, page 159, to paint Santa on canvas.

3. Paint beard lightly with iridescent glitter paint.
4. Cut shape from canvas.
5. For nose, paint peg red and glue to head.

COLOR KEY
☐ white
☐ flesh
☐ pink
☐ red
☐ blue
☐ grey
■ black

OLD ST. NICK

46

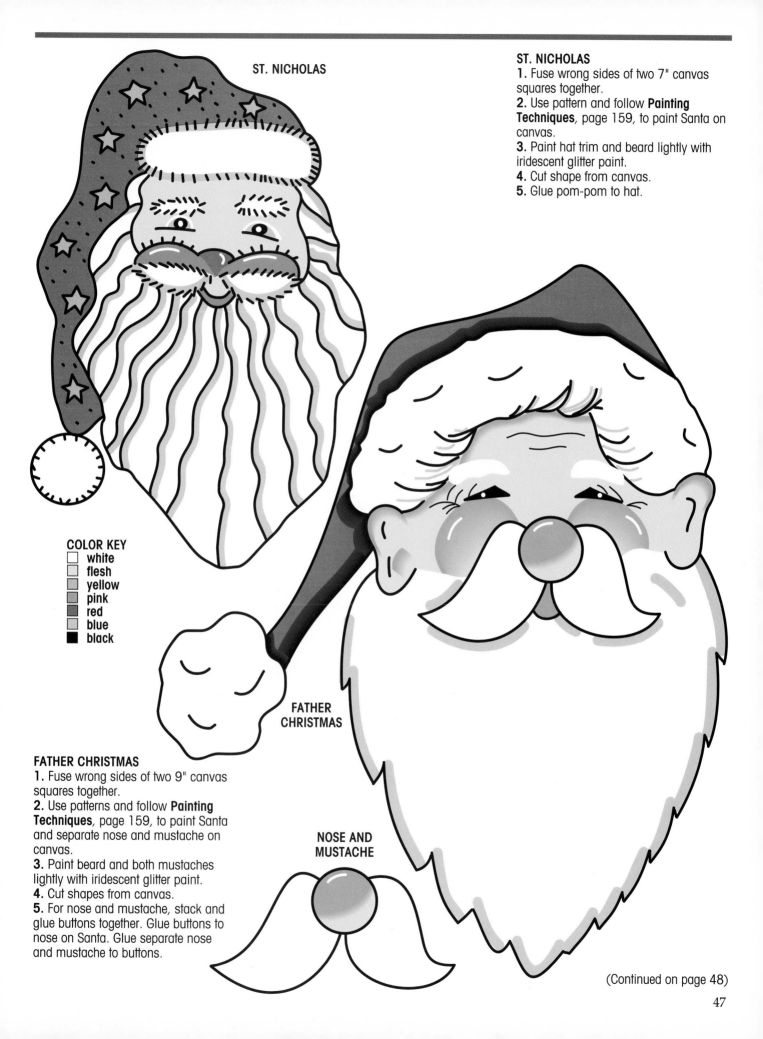

ST. NICHOLAS

ST. NICHOLAS
1. Fuse wrong sides of two 7" canvas squares together.
2. Use pattern and follow **Painting Techniques**, page 159, to paint Santa on canvas.
3. Paint hat trim and beard lightly with iridescent glitter paint.
4. Cut shape from canvas.
5. Glue pom-pom to hat.

COLOR KEY
☐ white
☐ flesh
☐ yellow
☐ pink
☐ red
☐ blue
■ black

FATHER
CHRISTMAS

FATHER CHRISTMAS
1. Fuse wrong sides of two 9" canvas squares together.
2. Use patterns and follow **Painting Techniques**, page 159, to paint Santa and separate nose and mustache on canvas.
3. Paint beard and both mustaches lightly with iridescent glitter paint.
4. Cut shapes from canvas.
5. For nose and mustache, stack and glue buttons together. Glue buttons to nose on Santa. Glue separate nose and mustache to buttons.

NOSE AND
MUSTACHE

(Continued on page 48)

PAINTED SANTAS (Continued)

SANTA CLAUS
1. Fuse wrong sides of two 10" canvas squares together.
2. Use patterns and follow **Painting Techniques**, page 159, to paint Santa, list, and sack on canvas.
3. Paint beard and buttons lightly with iridescent glitter paint.
4. Use pen to personalize list.
5. Cut shapes from canvas.
6. Glue list and sack to Santa's hands.

COLOR KEY
- white
- flesh
- pink
- red
- blue
- beige
- light brown
- brown
- black

SANTA CLAUS

LIST

SACK

48

GRANDFATHER FROST

1. Cut three 9" canvas squares (1 square is for coat). Fuse wrong sides of 2 canvas squares together.

2. Use patterns and follow **Painting Techniques**, page 159, to paint coat on right side of single canvas square; paint remaining parts on fused square.

3. Paint beard lightly with iridescent glitter paint. Paint star cutout yellow.

4. Cut shapes from canvas.

5. With short curved edge at top of cone half and straight edges overlapping at back (flat side), glue coat around cone half. Glue coat trim around bottom of cone half.

6. For socks, use utility knife to cut an approx. 1" long slit at center bottom of cone half. Glue socks into slit.

7. Glue eyebrows, mustache, and cuffs to upper body. Glue bead to mustache for nose. Glue upper body to cone half. Glue 1 end of pick to back of star and remaining end to mitten.

COLOR KEY
- white
- yellow
- flesh
- pink
- red
- green
- blue
- black

GRANDFATHER FROST

EYEBROWS

UPPER BODY

COAT

MUSTACHE

CUFFS

SOCKS

COAT TRIM

(Continued on page 50)

COLOR KEY
- ☐ white
- ☐ flesh
- ▨ pink
- ▨ red
- ▨ blue
- ▨ green
- ■ black

KRIS
KRINGLE

KRIS KRINGLE

1. Fuse wrong sides of two 10½" canvas squares together.
2. Use patterns and follow **Painting Techniques**, page 159, to paint Santa and letters on canvas.

3. Paint beard, hat trim, and coat trim lightly with iridescent glitter paint.
4. Cut shapes from canvas.
5. Use a needle to pierce a hole in each mitten. Thread needle with a 5" length of floss and thread floss loosely through holes. Glue ends of floss to backs of mittens. Glue letters to floss.

REINDEER FEED BAGS
(Shown on page 42)

For each bag, you will need a 6½" x 9" fabric piece, thread to match fabric, polyester fiberfill, white paper, serrated-cut craft scissors, black felt-tip pen, cotton string, and fabric glue.

1. For bag, match right sides and short edges and fold fabric in half. Using a ¼" seam allowance, sew raw edges together along 1 long and 1 short edge. Clip corners and turn bag right side out. Stuff with fiberfill to about 1" from top. Glue centers of raw edges at top of bag together.
2. Cut two 5" lengths of string. Knot 1 length around each top corner of bag.
3. For label, use craft scissors to cut a 1¾" x 3¼" piece of white paper. Use pen to write "Reindeer Feed" on label and draw stitches close to edges. Glue label to bag.

SANTA'S LIST ORNAMENTS
(Shown on page 42)

For each ornament, you will need fabric for leaves, fusible web, poster board, a 2¼" x 9¼" white paper strip, 9" of floral wire, red and black pens, tracing paper, wrapped peppermint candy, and a glue gun.

1. Fuse fabric to poster board.
2. Trace leaf pattern onto tracing paper; cut out.
3. Use pattern to cut 2 leaves from fabric-covered poster board.
4. For list, use pens to write names and draw check marks on paper strip. Glue wire length along center back of strip; curl strip as desired.
5. Glue leaves together. Glue candy to leaves. Glue top of list to back of leaves.

CHRISTMAS BOOTS (Shown on page 45)

For each boot, you will need two 13" x 17" fabric pieces for boot, fabric for leaf appliqués, synthetic fur for cuff, fusible web, black thread and thread to match boot fabric and fur, $^3/_4$ yd of $^3/_8$"w black grosgrain ribbon, acrylic paint (see color key, page 46 or 47), metallic gold dimensional paint, iridescent glitter fabric paint, paintbrushes, a palette, 4 assorted red buttons for berries, fabric marking pen, tracing paper, graphite transfer paper, toothpicks, paper towels, a piece of cardboard covered with waxed paper, removable tape, and fabric glue.

1. For boot pattern, match dotted lines and align arrows and trace top, heel, and toe of boot pattern onto tracing paper; cut out.
2. For boot, place boot fabric pieces right sides together. Use fabric marking pen to draw around pattern on fabric. Cutting $^1/_2$" outside drawn lines, cut out shapes.
3. Pin boot front fabric shape right side up on covered cardboard.

4. For Santa, use pattern, page 46 or 47, and follow **Painting Techniques**, page 159, to paint design on fabric piece.
5. Paint beard lightly with iridescent glitter paint.
6. For bootlaces, cut three 1$^3/_4$" lengths of ribbon. Glue ribbon lengths about $^1/_2$" apart along toe side of painted boot front. Use gold paint to paint a grommet at end of each ribbon length.
7. For leaf appliqués on toe of boot, use holly leaf pattern, page 50, and follow **Making Appliqués**, page 158, to make 2 leaves. Fuse leaves to boot. (Set aside paper backing from 1 leaf to use in Step 12.) Use black thread to sew 2 buttons to boot for berries.
8. Pin boot front and back fabric pieces right sides together. Leaving top edge open, sew front and back together along drawn lines. Clip seam allowance.
9. To hem top, press edge $^1/_2$" to wrong side and stitch in place. Turn boot right side out and press.

10. For cuff, measure around top of boot and add 1". Cut a piece of fur 3$^1/_2$" wide by the determined measurement. Matching right sides and short edges, fold cuff in half. Using a $^1/_2$" seam allowance, sew short edges together to form a tube; turn right side out.
11. Slip cuff over top of boot and center cuff seam at center back of boot. Using a $^1/_2$" seam allowance, sew cuff to boot.
12. For leaves on cuff, cut two 5" fabric squares. Fuse fabric squares wrong sides together. Using paper backing from holly leaf appliqué as a pattern, cut 2 leaves from fused fabric.
13. Use black thread to sew leaves to cuff. Sew remaining buttons to cuff.
14. For hanger on boot, press each end of a 4$^1/_2$" ribbon length $^1/_2$" to 1 side. Matching folded ends, fold ribbon in half to form a loop. Sew ends of loop inside boot at heel-side seam.
15. Tie remaining ribbon into a bow; trim ends. Use black thread to sew bow to boot above laces.

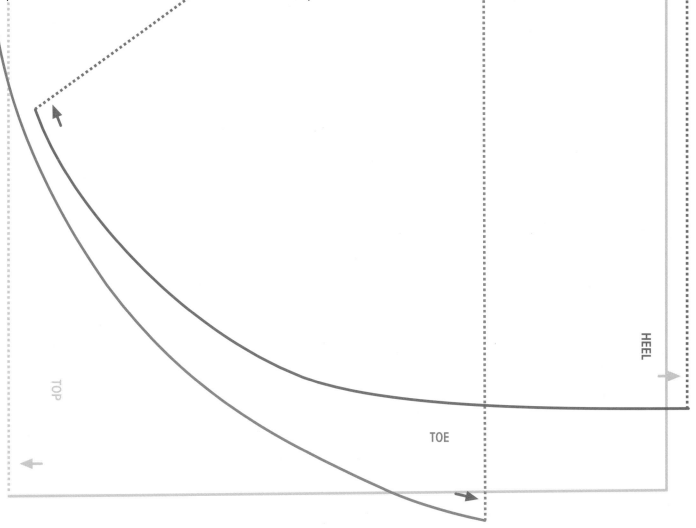

TOP

HEEL

TOE

SANTA COLLECTOR SWEATSHIRT AND SIGN (Shown on pages 44 and 45)

You will need fabrics for letter appliqués, fusible web, acrylic paint (see color key, page 53), iridescent glitter fabric paint, paintbrushes, a palette, black permanent felt-tip pen, tracing paper, graphite transfer paper, small sharp scissors, toothpicks, and paper towels.

For sweatshirt, you will **also** need a sweatshirt large enough for a 10" x 19" design, assorted buttons, jingle bells, clear nylon thread, thread for buttons and bells, and a T-shirt form or cardboard covered with waxed paper.

For sign, you will **also** need a 12" x 24" canvas panel and frame to hold panel, fabric for leaf appliqués, 1¼ yds of 2½"w wired red ribbon, cream acrylic paint for background, small sponge piece, berries cut from a silk berry pick, pressing cloth, and a glue gun.

SWEATSHIRT

1. For letters, follow **Making Appliqués**, page 158, to make letters to spell "santa collector." For bottom layers of letter appliqués, fuse web to wrong sides of fabrics. Fuse letters to fabrics. Cutting close to outer edges of letters and even with openings, cut letters from fabrics.

2. Fuse letters to shirt. Use nylon thread and follow **Machine Appliqué**, page 158, to stitch over edges of appliqués.

3. Insert T-shirt form into shirt.

4. For Santas, use patterns, this page and page 53, and follow **Painting Techniques**, page 159, to paint designs on shirt.

5. Paint beards lightly with iridescent glitter paint.

6. Sew a bell to point of each hat. Sew buttons to shirt.

SIGN

1. (**Note:** Refer to **Painting Techniques**, page 159, for painting steps.) Apply cream basecoat to canvas panel. Sponge paint white paint around edges.

2. For letters, follow Step 1 of Sweatshirt instructions. Use pressing cloth to fuse letters to panel. Use pen to draw stitches around letters.

3. For Santas, use patterns, this page and page 53, to paint designs on panel.

4. Paint beards lightly with iridescent glitter paint.

5. Use leaf pattern and follow **Making Appliqués**, page 158, to make 20 leaves. Use pressing cloth to fuse leaves to panel.

6. Glue berries to panel for berries and noses on Santas.

7. Secure panel in frame.

8. Tie ribbon into a bow; trim ends. Glue to frame.

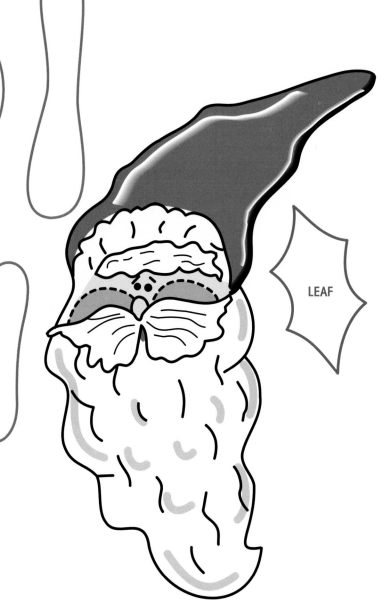

LEAF

COLOR KEY

☐ white
☐ flesh
☐ pink
☐ red
☐ blue
☐ grey
■ black

SHUTTER CARD HOLDER
(Shown on page 43)

You will need a wooden shutter (ours is 15" x 39"), assorted fabrics for trim, fusible web, green spray paint, 6 large buttons, pressing cloth, glue gun, 1 Santa Claus (page 48), and 1 Grandfather Frost (page 49).

1. (**Note:** Bottom of shutter is top of card holder.) Spray paint shutter green.
2. For fabric trim on shutter, fuse web to wrong sides of fabrics. Measure flat areas at top, center, bottom, and sides of front of shutter. Cut fabric strips slightly smaller on all sides than measured areas. Using pressing cloth, fuse fabric strips to shutter, overlapping ends as necessary.
3. Glue Santas and buttons to shutter.

JOLLY GIFT BAG
(Shown on page 43)

You will need a small gift bag, ²/₃ yd each of ⁷/₈"w and ¹/₂"w satin ribbon, 6" of ¹/₈"w satin ribbon, hole punch, glue gun, and 1 St. Nicholas (page 47).

1. Fold top of bag about 1¹/₂" to front.
2. Punch 2 holes close together at center of folded part of bag.
3. Thread ⁷/₈"w and ¹/₂"w ribbons through holes and tie into a bow at front of bag; trim ends.
4. For ornament hanger, fold ¹/₈"w ribbon in half to form a loop and glue ends to back of Santa. Place loop over bow on bag.

SANTA CLAUS T-SHIRT
(Shown on page 44)

You will need a shirt large enough for a 9" x 8" design, acrylic paint (see color key, page 48), iridescent glitter fabric paint, paintbrushes, a palette, black permanent felt-tip pen, tracing paper, graphite transfer paper or dressmakers' tracing paper, paper towels, and a T-shirt form or cardboard covered with waxed paper.

1. Use patterns, page 48, and follow **Painting Techniques**, page 159, to paint designs on shirt.
2. Paint beard and buttons lightly with iridescent glitter paint.
3. Use pen to personalize list.

A MEDLEY OF MANTELS

An ordinary fireplace mantel can become a festive focal point with a few creative touches. It's easy to re-create any one of our merry montages using crafted accents and items you already have on hand, such as candle holders, crystal stemware, fruit, and dried naturals. Our spectacular designs include elegant finishes in gold and silver, traditional arrangements with lush evergreens, and an old-fashioned display with homespun appeal. Even if you don't have a mantel, you can still use these inviting ideas to fashion one-of-a-kind centerpieces for the dining room table or buffet, as well as to dress up a china cabinet or bookshelf. Instructions for these projects begin on page 58.

Reflecting the opulence of Christmas, the **All That Glitters Mantel** *(page 58)* features sparkling dried naturals, glass ball ornaments, and gilded silk roses among greenery. *(Opposite, top)* Our **Gilded Naturals Mantel** *(page 60)* is unpretentiously elegant with swirls of grapevine bathed in gold. Papier-mâché reindeer and natural topiaries touched with silver and copper also grace the mantel. *(Opposite, bottom)* A resplendent display for your Nativity, our **Away in a Manger Mantel** *(page 60)* begins with a metallic wreath hung above the Holy Family. A star and shimmering ribbons cascade down and around the figures, and rich folds of tapestry fabric, poinsettias, and framed lines from a favorite carol complete the divine scene.

Loaded with charming trims from fresh apple candle holders to potpourri-filled canning jars, the **Homespun and Spice Mantel** *(page 59)* is a nice way to showcase old-fashioned treasures. Cinnamony angel ornaments and fresh cedar branches add an aromatic touch, and a kitchen-towel mantel scarf and sock stockings are delightful accents, too. *(Opposite, top)* For a Colonial Christmas, try our **Williamsburg Mantel** *(page 61)*. Fresh gilded fruit and a stately pineapple are prominently displayed atop a tier of boxwood, cedar, and pine. Handsome partridge-in-a-pear-tree topiaries in antiqued urns regally flank each end of the mantel. *(Opposite, bottom)* The **Holly and Ivy Mantel** *(page 58)* offers a timeless arrangement of fresh greenery, brass candle holders fitted with red tapers, and brilliant poinsettias. Handmade stockings with velvet cuffs are hung from the mantel for a classic finish.

ALL THAT GLITTERS MANTEL (Shown on page 54)

A sophisticated use of crystal, glass, and brass that you already have on hand is the idea behind the exquisite display of glimmering gold and white atop this mantel.

To begin the grand arrangement, we gathered various sizes of brass and crystal candlesticks, glass stemware, and large and small glass bowls.

To enhance the sumptuous look of the majestic antique mirror already in place at the center of the mantel, we filled a large glass bowl with various sizes of gleaming gold ball ornaments and added a sunburst of gold grasses, fronds, and leaves and a pair of gilded white silk roses. We placed the large bowl on top of a smaller bowl for height and placed it to one side of the mirror for an asymmetrical arrangement.

We wrapped bricks in fabric and placed them on the mantel to support the varying sizes of crystal and glistening brass candlesticks we had gathered. To achieve exactly the right height for some of the candles, we used inverted stemware for stands. We used pure white and ivory pillar and taper candles, some tied with luxurious gold cords and others with sparkling wired white ribbon bows. On some of the ribbon-wrapped candles, we tucked small pieces of gold grass behind the bows.

The greenery is a silk garland we cut into pieces and draped among the candlesticks, crystal, and stemware. Woven into the greenery is a twinkling garland of gold and crystal beads. We purchased long-stemmed ivory silk roses embellished with gold edges and tucked them among the greenery, bending the stems as necessary to conceal them.

To echo the lustrous silk roses, our lovely Painted Rose Ornaments feature white roses on golden matte glass ornaments. The ornaments are suspended from lengths of wired white ribbon taped to the mantel under the greenery, and we tied oversize bows of the same ribbon just above the ornaments. The pretty painted ornaments are a lavish finishing touch to the dazzling display on this mantel.

PAINTED ROSE ORNAMENTS

For each ornament, you will need a 3" dia. matte gold glass ball ornament, gold glitter and iridescent white dimensional paint, tracing paper, removable tape, and carbon paper.

1. Trace rose pattern onto tracing paper; cut out pattern just outside design.
2. Cut a piece of carbon paper same size as pattern. Place carbon paper and pattern on ornament and tape in place, clipping edges as necessary for pattern to lie flat. Trace over pattern to transfer design to ornament. Remove pattern and carbon paper.
3. Use gold glitter paint to paint over transferred lines.
4. Spreading paint thickly, use iridescent white paint to fill in petals of rose design and paint around leaves.

HOLLY AND IVY MANTEL (Shown on page 57)

What could be more fitting during this special season than bringing together holly and ivy, luxurious poinsettias, classic brass candlesticks, jingling brass bells, and a golden garland — a handsome group of Christmas favorites to adorn any mantel.

We began by placing poinsettias in large brass pots found at a local craft store. A collection of antique brass candlesticks with bright red candles were added for heartwarming appeal. We tied jingle bells to the ends of black satin ribbon lengths and tied the ribbons around the bottoms of the candlesticks.

We cut holly and ivy pieces from potted plants and outdoors and placed the cuttings in small floral containers filled with water to keep them fresh throughout the season (the containers are available at florist's shops).

Carefully concealing the containers at the back of the mantel, we draped the holly and ivy along the length of the mantel, allowing some of the tendrils to hang over the edge. Among the greenery, we placed large brass jingle bells and a golden rope garland with bright red beads.

The Regal Stockings are another classic touch. Made from plaid corduroy cut on the bias, the stockings have deep cuffs of black velvet and cheery jingle bells.

REGAL STOCKINGS

For each stocking, you will need 9" of ¹/₂"w ribbon for hanger, thread to match fabrics, jingle bells, fabric marking pen, and tracing paper.

For each large stocking, you will **also** need two 12" x 18" fabric pieces for stocking (or two 18" x 20" fabric pieces to cut stocking on the bias) and one 12¹/₂" x 17" fabric piece for cuff.

For small stocking, you will **also** need two 9" x 13" fabric pieces for stocking (or two 12¹/₂" x 16" fabric pieces to cut stocking on the bias), one 8¹/₂" x 13" fabric piece for cuff, and copier paper.

LARGE STOCKING

1. Matching dotted lines and aligning arrows, trace top and bottom of stocking pattern, page 18, onto tracing paper; cut out.
2. (**Note:** If making stocking on the bias, place pattern on fabric bias for Step 2.) Leaving top edge open and cutting along drawn line at top of stocking, follow **Sewing Shapes**, page 158, to make stocking from stocking fabric pieces.
3. (**Note:** Use a ¹/₂" seam allowance for remaining sewing steps.) For cuff, match right sides and short edges and fold cuff in half. Sew short edges together to form a tube; press seam allowance open. Matching wrong sides and raw edges, fold tube in half.
4. To attach cuff to stocking, place cuff inside stocking with seamline of cuff at center back and matching raw edges; pin cuff to stocking. Sew cuff to stocking. Pull cuff out and fold down over stocking.
5. For hanger, fold ribbon length in half to form a loop. Sew ends inside stocking close to heel-side seamline.
6. Spacing evenly, sew bells to bottom edge of cuff.

SMALL STOCKING

1. For stocking pattern, follow Step 1 of Large Stocking instructions. Use copy machine to reduce pattern to 77% of its original size; cut out pattern.
2. To complete stocking, follow Steps 2 - 6 of Large Stocking instructions.

HOMESPUN AND SPICE MANTEL (Shown on page 56)

We brought together the warmth, coziness, and wonderful smells of an old-fashioned Christmas with this charming display of old and new treasures sure to bring back memories of long ago holidays. Raid your kitchen cabinets, your grandmother's cabinets, or your nearby antique store for mementos similar to the ones we found. We used measuring cups, canning jars filled with spices and dried fruit slices, and shiny red apples and pressed tiny tart pans into service as candleholders. We used baking pans to place some of the items at different levels on the mantel to create interest and to better display them.

The heartwarming Mantel Scarf is the foundation for the arrangement. Made from plaid kitchen towels, the edges are simply cut and fused to form the points.

For a centerpiece, we placed a folksy wire tree on an aluminum loaf pan. For the crisp red apple candleholders, we cut holes in the apples to fit each candle. Our garlands are strings of real popcorn and cranberries.

We hung our fragrant Cinnamon Angels, made with a dough of applesauce and cinnamon, on the purchased aluminum candlesticks.

Aromatic cinnamon sticks and fresh greenery boughs add festive touches to this informal arrangement.

To complete the look, we hung our Simple Stockings from the mantel. For these we simply fused fabric hearts to coffee-dyed socks.

CINNAMON ANGELS

For 3 angels, you will need ground cinnamon (we used most of a 4 oz. container), applesauce, jute twine for hangers, tracing paper, paring knife, and a glue gun.

1. Trace head, heart, and wing patterns separately onto tracing paper; cut out.
2. Mix 11 tablespoons of cinnamon and 6 tablespoons of warm applesauce together to form a smooth dough. If dough is too soft to work with easily, add more cinnamon; if too stiff, add more applesauce. Divide dough into thirds.
3. (**Note:** Spread aluminum foil over work surface. Follow Steps 3 - 6 for each angel.) Pat 1/3 of dough out with fingers until it is about 1/4" thick.
4. Place patterns on dough and use knife to cut out shapes. Use fingers to smooth edges.
5. Place head and heart on wings and gently press pieces together. Allow to dry 2 to 3 days.
6. For hanger, cut a 7" length of twine. Fold twine in half and glue ends to top back of angel.

SIMPLE STOCKINGS

For each stocking, you will need 1 men's white sock with red toe, heel, and ribbing; fabric for appliqués; fusible web; tracing paper; 16" of craft wire; and instant coffee.

1. To coffee-dye sock, dissolve 2 tablespoons coffee in 2 cups hot water; allow to cool. Soak sock in coffee several minutes; remove from coffee, allow to dry, and press.
2. Use heart pattern and follow **Making Appliqués**, page 158, to make 3 heart appliqués. Fuse appliqués to sock.
3. For hanger, push ends of craft wire through sides of ribbing; bend ends up and twist to secure.

MANTEL SCARF

For each section of mantel scarf (we used 2 sections for our mantel), you will need a 20" x 27 1/2" kitchen towel, 1/2"w fusible web tape, and a fabric marking pen.

1. (**Note:** Each scarf section has 2 points. Follow all steps for each section.) Match short edges and fold towel in half; mark center of each long edge. Use fabric marking pen to draw a line on wrong side of towel connecting marks. Draw a second line 7" from 1 long edge of towel (bottom edge).
2. Fuse web tape along bottom edge on wrong side of towel, along side edges from horizontal line to first piece of web tape, and on each side of line at center from horizontal line to first piece of web tape (**Fig. 1**).

Fig. 1

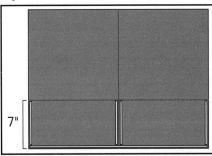

3. Cut along center line up to horizontal line. Mark center bottom of each section.
4. Fold side edges of each section to wrong side from horizontal line to marked center point; fuse in place (**Fig. 2**).

Fig. 2

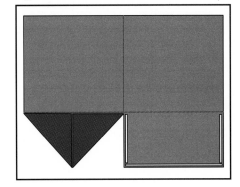

AWAY IN A MANGER MANTEL (Shown on page 55)

To enhance your own precious Nativity figurines, we suggest you adapt this exquisite arrangement to your mantel.

We began by covering a box (a large shoe box works well) with resplendent red and gold fabric, tucking and arranging the fabric to our liking.

Trailing streams of glory, the Christmas star appears above the babe in the manger. To achieve the celestial effect, we used a 24" dia. grapevine wreath, which becomes a glorious accent when painted with metallic gold spray paint. (We placed our wreath on the box behind the figurines, but you may want to hang the wreath over the mantel.) We wired a length of gold netting to the wreath, gathering 1 end at the top and arranging the bottom of the netting over the fabric-covered box. We fastened a bow tied from a long length of 4"w sheer golden ribbon to the top of the wreath over the netting and glued a 6" gold star ornament under the bow.

An opulent gold and scarlet rope garland and gold, scarlet, and black bead garlands were intertwined and woven along the length of the mantel. For a touch of dramatic color, we also added luxuriant mauve silk poinsettias and red and gold glass ball ornaments.

We used a calligraphy pen to copy the words from a child's favorite Christmas hymn onto pieces of parchment paper and placed the verses in small gold frames. Arranged among the folds of fabric on the mantel, the words of the carol are a sweet remembrance.

Finally, nestled into the heart of all the loveliness, we placed the ceramic figurines, fastening them with masking tape to the top of the box to keep them secure.

GILDED NATURALS MANTEL (Shown on page 55)

Gathering natural bounty (maybe from your own backyard or neighborhood) and using paint to burnish all the found items is the plan behind this glowing mantel. We set an abundance of natural elements "afire" by burnishing them with gleaming gold, lustrous silver, and shimmering copper paint.

The Gilded Topiaries are made by placing a pre-shaped topiary form and a large plastic foam ball into gold- and silver-painted flowerpots and covering them with glossy painted pinecones and nuts. We also spray painted a grapevine topiary gold, wound silver ribbon around it, and placed it on the mantel in a flowerpot saucer painted gold.

For a focal point, we spray painted 12" and 15" papier-mâché deer gold and placed them at the center of the mantel.

More painted pinecones and nuts like the ones in our topiaries were added around the topiaries and deer for additional sparkle. Strands of grapevine and grapevine balls, also lightly sprayed gold, were draped and arranged along the length of the mantel. For a pleasing final touch, we wound more of the silver mesh ribbon among all the glimmering richness.

GILDED TOPIARIES
You will need assorted pinecones (our pinecones range in length from about ³/₄" to 2¹/₂"); assorted nuts (we used walnuts, brazil nuts, hazelnuts, almonds, and pecans); sheet moss; sphagnum moss; metallic gold, silver, and copper spray paint; metallic gold acrylic paint; paintbrush; spray primer; spray adhesive; ³/₄"w masking tape; and a glue gun.
For cone topiary, you will **also** need a 7" dia. clay flowerpot, a 22"h plastic foam cone topiary form, and 1¹/₄ yds of 1³/₈"w silver mesh ribbon.
For round topiary, you will **also** need a 5¹/₂" dia. clay flowerpot and a 6" dia. plastic foam ball.

CONE TOPIARY
1. Spray flowerpot with primer. Spray paint pot silver.
2. Place lengths of masking tape about 2" apart around pot (**Fig. 1**). Spray paint pot gold. After paint is dry, carefully remove masking tape.

Fig. 1

3. Spray paint large pinecones gold. Spray paint some small pinecones copper (we left some of our small pinecones natural). Spray paint nuts silver. Dilute gold acrylic paint with water. Use diluted paint and paintbrush to lightly paint nuts gold.
4. Crumble sheet moss on work surface. Spray cone with spray adhesive. Completely covering cone, roll cone in sheet moss.
5. Glue bottom of topiary form into pot. Glue sphagnum moss over top of topiary form base. Glue several pinecones to moss.
6. Completely covering cone, hot glue pinecones and nuts to cone as desired.
7. Tie ribbon into a bow around trunk; trim ends.

ROUND TOPIARY
1. Spacing lengths of masking tape about 1¹/₂" apart on pot, follow Steps 1 - 3 of Cone Topiary instructions.
2. Glue foam ball to top of flowerpot.
3. To complete topiary, follow Steps 5 and 6 of Cone Topiary instructions.

Christmas is a time of filling our homes with the best of nature's bounty and sharing it with all who come to our doors. In the tradition of our forefathers who decorated their homes with natural beauty and welcomed their neighbors to share in its richness, we offer this mantel, abounding with luxuriant fruits and splendid greenery.

As a base for this plentiful arrangement, we used sheets of plastic foam to build up three tiered levels. Leaving room for the topiaries at each end of the mantel, we measured the rest of the mantel and cut one large piece of foam. We cut another piece of foam about 3" smaller on the sides and front and a third smaller piece for the pineapple centerpiece and placed them on the first piece. We folded pieces of floral wire in half and pushed the ends into the foam pieces to secure all the pieces together. We then sprayed the foam pieces with spray adhesive and covered them with sheet moss. The cedar, pine, and boxwood greenery is attached to the foam pieces using greening pins.

For the pinecone picks, we wired small pinecones to bundles of twigs, attached them to wired floral picks, and speared the picks into the foam base.

For the pineapple centerpiece, we folded a length of heavy floral wire in half and inserted the ends into the bottom of the pineapple and the fold into the center top of the foam base.

All the abundant display of fruit is real. We used Washington Red and green pears, purple plums, red apples, oranges, lemons, and bunches of purple and white grapes. For each piece of large fruit, we inserted a piece of heavy wire through the center of the fruit, bent the ends of the wire to secure the fruit (see **Fig. 3** below), and securely inserted the ends of the wire into the foam base. The bunches of grapes were attached to the foam with more greening pins. For additional color, we added small artificial berry picks to the arrangement.

For a rich finish, we added natural highlights to the fruit, picks, and greenery by lightly painting them with diluted gold paint.

PARTRIDGE AND PEARS TOPIARIES

For each topiary, you will need an 8"h plastic urn; desired fruit and greenery (we used Washington Red and green pears, red grapes, and boxwood); 1 approx. 6"h artificial partridge; magnolia leaves; a 15"h plastic foam cone; 2 plastic foam disks to fit in top of urn (we used 1³/₁₆" x 5⁷/₈" disks); floral foam brick; metallic gold, green, and black spray paint; metallic gold acrylic paint; paintbrush; wood-tone spray; spray adhesive; heavy floral wire; wire cutters; greening pins; sheet moss; sand; and a glue gun.

1. Spray paint urn black. Lightly spray urn alternately with green paint, wood-tone spray, and gold paint until urn has a bronzed appearance. Use gold acrylic paint and paintbrush to lightly paint edges and to highlight urn.
2. Trim foam brick to fit inside urn; glue to secure.
3. Place foam disks on top of brick in urn. Fold pieces of floral wire in half and push ends into disks to secure disks to brick.
4. To weight urn, pour sand into urn to top of foam disks.
5. Glue a small amount of sheet moss to urn to cover rim.
6. Trim about 1¹/₂" from 1 end of each magnolia leaf. Overlapping cut ends, glue leaves around rim of urn (**Fig. 1**).

Fig. 1

7. Crumble sheet moss on work surface. Spray cone with spray adhesive. Completely covering cone, roll cone in sheet moss.
8. To secure cone to urn, insert 3 wire lengths into bottom of cone and disks in urn (**Fig. 2**).

Fig. 2

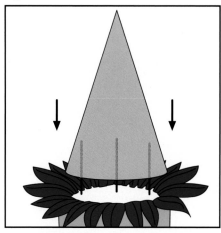

9. To attach pears to topiary, insert a wire length through widest part of each pear. Bend ends of wire to secure fruit (**Fig. 3**). Spacing fruit as desired, push ends of wire into cone.

Fig. 3

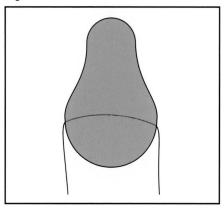

10. For greenery, use greening pins to secure pieces of greenery to cone, completely filling in around fruit.
11. Use pick on partridge to insert bird into top of cone; glue to secure.
12. Use greening pins to secure small bunches of grapes to bottom of cone on top of magnolia leaves.
13. Use diluted gold paint to paint highlights on topiary.

CHEERY FELT CHARMERS

*O*ur ever-so-friendly snow couple extends an open-arms welcome to holiday guests in this winsome collection of felt decorations. Miniature versions of the plump pair add cheery appeal to the evergreen, which is displayed in an old-fashioned washtub. The tree is wrapped with a scalloped garland of green felt and adorned with flower, heart, star, and cottage ornaments. A warm, fuzzy blanket, colorful stockings, and tabletop topiaries will also give your Christmas celebration a down-home country spin! Instructions for the projects shown here and on the following pages begin on page 68.

Our adorable **Snow Folks** *(page 71)* beckon holiday guests to warm themselves near the fire. Stuffed with fiberfill, the larger-than-life friends are embellished with blanket stitching and buttons. The cheery gentleman offers a big "hello" with outstretched twig arms and blue mitten hands, and the missus totes a basket of pretty posies.

Covered with homespun charm, our **Cheery Felt Charmers Tree** *(page 68)* is trimmed with a host of felt cuties. The little stuffed **From-the-Heart Ornaments** *(page 68)* include cottages, stars, flowers, hearts, and miniature snow people. A wooden bead garland and wide "ruffles" of green felt are draped among the branches. Giant pewter jingle bells and miniature white candles in tin holders complete the folksy look.

Add a playful fashion accessory to your holiday wardrobe with our **Snowy Day Vest** *(page 73)*. A sawtooth pattern is cut along the edges of the black felt lining for a decorative finish.

These **Mini Felt Evergreens** *(page 72)* make merry mantel decorations, especially when arranged with fresh greenery, candles, and jingle bells. Displayed in metal pails, the topiaries are created by wrapping strips of felt around plastic foam cones.

Trimmed with colorful appliqués, running stitches, and button borders, **Sweet Felt Stockings** *(page 73)* are cute additions to the mantel — or anywhere they're displayed. The back panels are cut a little larger than the fronts to create the old-fashioned sawtooth edging. *(Opposite)* For the **Snow Folks Cover-up** *(page 72)*, a plain woolen afghan is dressed up with our enchanting couple. The felt appliqués are created by enlarging the ornament patterns on a photocopier and blanket stitching the cutouts onto the cozy throw.

CHEERY FELT CHARMERS
TREE (Shown on page 63)

Blanketed with strips of cozy green felt and covered with whimsical felt ornaments, this colorful 7½-foot-tall tree is a truly heartwarming addition to the holidays.

As a unique backdrop for our richly hued ornaments, we cut scalloped edges on felt strips and layered them among the branches. Our strips range from 5½" wide at the top of the tree to about 10" wide at the bottom. A wooden bead garland, large pewter jingle bells, and small white candles in shiny tin holders add to the informality of the evergreen (the candles are for decorative use only).

As easy to make as they are charming, the From-the-Heart Ornaments (this page) include smiling snow folks, cute cottages, colorful hearts, simple stars, and pretty flowers. Fun touches on the ornaments include easy embroidery stitches and small buttons.

To complete the folksy look, we placed our evergreen in a large galvanized tub, packed the tub with newspaper, and covered the newspaper with a layer of sphagnum moss. The pretty packages beneath the tree are wrapped with bright felt bows.

FROM-THE-HEART
ORNAMENTS (Shown on page 64)

You will need assorted colors of felt (we used ivory, yellow, dark yellow, red, dark red, blue, green, dark green, tan, and brown), polyester fiberfill, assorted colors of embroidery floss (we used ivory, green, tan, brown, and black), embroidery needle, assorted small buttons, tracing paper, and fabric glue.
For each snow woman or snowman ornament, you will **also** need ivory and orange felt and black embroidery floss.
For each snowman ornament, you will **also** need two 3½" long wooden craft picks for arms.

Note: Cut 1 shape unless instructed otherwise on pattern. Refer to **Embroidery** instructions, page 158, for embroidery. Use 2 strands of floss for embroidery and to sew on buttons unless otherwise indicated. If floss color is not specified, use any color.

SNOW WOMAN ORNAMENT
1. Trace snow woman ornament patterns, page 69, onto tracing paper; cut out.
2. Use patterns to cut 2 body shapes from ivory felt and nose from orange felt. Cut remaining shapes from other colors of felt.
3. Use black floss to work French Knots for eyes and Running Stitch for mouth on 1 body shape.
4. Work Running Stitch along center of each large leaf for vein. Glue nose and leaves to snow woman, overlapping leaves. Sew a button to leaves at overlap.
5. To assemble snow woman, place body shapes together. Leaving an opening for stuffing, use black floss to work Blanket Stitch along edges of shapes. Stuff body lightly with fiberfill; stitch opening closed.
6. For basket, place shapes together and work Blanket Stitch along edges of handle and outer edges of basket. Arrange daisies and small leaves on basket; glue in place. Sew a button to center of each daisy. Tack basket handle to 1 side of snow woman.
7. Center hat on back of head and work Running Stitch around center of hat to secure.

SNOWMAN ORNAMENT
1. Use snowman ornament patterns, page 69, and follow Steps 1 - 3 of Snow Woman Ornament instructions.
2. Glue nose to snowman. Sew 3 buttons along center of snowman.
3. For each arm, place 2 mitten shapes together and work Running Stitch along edges, leaving straight edge unstitched. Glue 1 end of 1 pick inside mitten. Glue remaining end of pick to wrong side on 1 side of snowman front.
4. To assemble snowman, follow Step 5 of Snow Woman Ornament instructions.
5. For vest, work Blanket Stitch along edges of vest shapes. Glue shapes to snowman.
6. For hat, glue top of head between bottom edges of folded hat. Work Running Stitch through all layers close to bottom edges of hat.
7. Glue daisy and leaf to 1 side of hat. Sew a button to center of daisy.

STAR ORNAMENT
1. Trace star ornament patterns, page 70, onto tracing paper; cut out.
2. Use patterns to cut shapes from felt.

3. For veins on leaves, work Straight Stitches along center of each leaf. Glue leaves, posy, and posy center to 1 star shape. Sew a button to posy center.
4. To assemble ornament, use star shapes and follow Step 5 of Snow Woman Ornament instructions.

COTTAGE ORNAMENT
1. Trace cottage ornament patterns, page 70, onto tracing paper; cut out.
2. Use patterns to cut shapes from felt.
3. Glue remaining shapes except chimney to folded cottage shape.
4. Sewing through front of ornament only, work long stitches on window for windowpanes. Using 6 strands of floss, sew a button to door for doorknob; sew a button to heart, knotting and trimming floss at front of button.
5. For chimney, place shapes together and work Running Stitch close to edges. For smoke, use 6 strands of floss and take a small stitch at top of chimney. Unthread needle, knot floss, and trim ends about 1½" from chimney. Glue bottom of chimney to wrong side of cottage front on 1 side of roof.
6. To assemble ornament, work Running Stitch close to side and roof edges of cottage, leaving an opening for stuffing. Stuff cottage lightly with fiberfill; stitch opening closed.

HEART ORNAMENT
1. Trace heart ornament patterns, page 70, onto tracing paper; cut out.
2. Use patterns to cut shapes from felt.
3. Glue small heart to ornament front.
4. Use 6 strands of floss to sew buttons to ornament front, knotting and trimming floss at front of buttons.
5. To assemble ornament, center ornament front on ornament back. Leaving an opening for stuffing, work Running Stitch close to edges of ornament front. Stuff heart lightly with fiberfill; stitch opening closed.

POSY OR DAISY ORNAMENTS
1. Trace desired flower and leaf patterns, page 71, onto tracing paper; cut out.
2. Use patterns to cut shapes from felt.
3. Glue posy centers to posies.
4. Sew button(s) to flower center(s).
5. For each leaf, glue leaf to a contrasting color of felt (we used ivory). For veins on leaf, work Running Stitch along center. Cutting close to leaf, cut leaf from felt. Glue leaves to back(s) of flower(s).

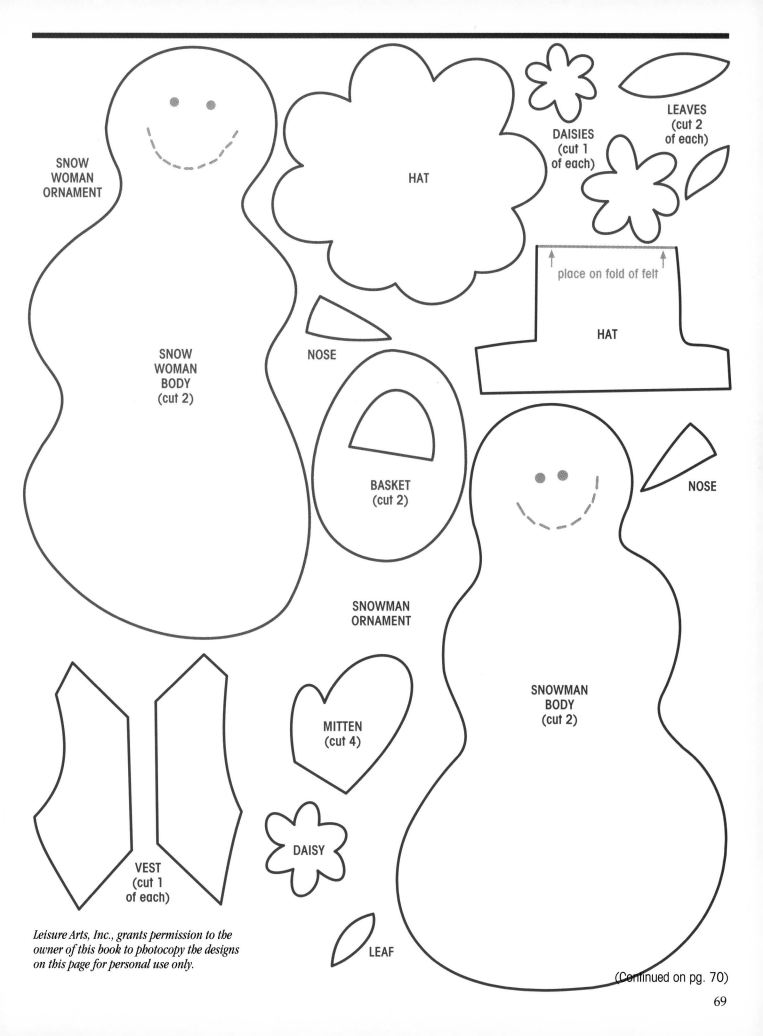

SNOW
WOMAN
ORNAMENT

SNOW
WOMAN
BODY
(cut 2)

HAT

DAISIES
(cut 1
of each)

LEAVES
(cut 2
of each)

place on fold of felt

HAT

NOSE

BASKET
(cut 2)

NOSE

SNOWMAN
ORNAMENT

SNOWMAN
BODY
(cut 2)

VEST
(cut 1
of each)

MITTEN
(cut 4)

DAISY

LEAF

(Continued on pg. 70)

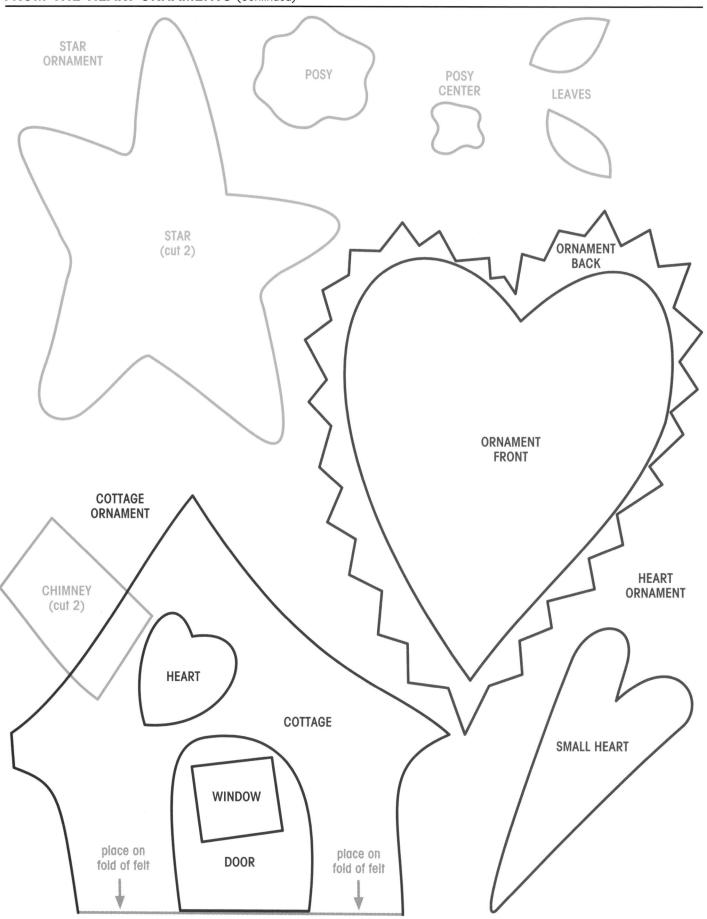

STAR
ORNAMENT

POSY

POSY
CENTER

LEAVES

STAR
(cut 2)

ORNAMENT
BACK

ORNAMENT
FRONT

COTTAGE
ORNAMENT

CHIMNEY
(cut 2)

HEART

COTTAGE

HEART
ORNAMENT

SMALL HEART

WINDOW

place on
fold of felt

place on
fold of felt

DOOR

SNOW FOLKS (Shown on page 62)

You will need ⅔ yd of 60"w ivory felt for snow woman and snowman, orange and assorted colors of felt (we used dark yellow, red, blue, green, dark green, and brown), polyester fiberfill, assorted buttons, black and assorted colors of embroidery floss (we used ivory, green, tan, and brown), embroidery needle, transparent tape (if needed), and fabric glue.
For Snowman you will **also** need two ¼" dia. 10" long twigs for arms.

1. To enlarge patterns for snow folks, photocopy snow woman and snowman ornament patterns, page 69, once at 200% and again at 129% (if necessary, cut and tape paper pieces together to form whole patterns); cut out.
2. (**Note:** Cut 1 shape unless instructed otherwise on pattern. Refer to **Embroidery** instructions, page 158, for embroidery. Use 3 strands of floss for embroidery and to sew on buttons unless otherwise indicated. If floss color is not specified,

use any color.) To assemble snow woman, follow Steps 2 - 7 of Snow Woman Ornament instructions, page 68.
3. To assemble snowman, use 2 layers of felt for each side of vest, use twigs for arms, and follow Steps 2 and 3 of Snow Woman Ornament instructions and Steps 2 - 7 of Snowman Ornament instructions, page 68.

SNOW FOLKS COVER-UP (Shown on page 67)

You will need either an approx. 61" x 42" pre-laundered wool fabric piece and thread to match or an approx. 61" x 42" purchased pre-laundered wool afghan, 1/2 yd of 60"w ivory felt for snow folks, orange and assorted colors of felt (we used dark yellow, red, blue, green, dark green, and brown), black and assorted colors of embroidery floss (we used green, tan, and brown), black yarn, embroidery needle, large needle, assorted buttons, transparent tape (if needed), fabric glue, and several Posy or Daisy Ornaments (page 68).

1. (**Note:** If purchased afghan is used, begin with Step 2.) To finish edges of wool fabric piece, use matching thread and a wide zigzag stitch with a short stitch length to stitch over edges.
2. Wash, dry, and press felt pieces.
3. To enlarge patterns for snow folks, follow Step 1 of Snow Folks instructions, page 71.
4. Use patterns to cut 1 snow woman and 1 snowman body shape from ivory felt and 1 of each nose from orange felt. Cut the following additional shapes from felt for snow woman: 2 baskets, 1 of each flower, 2 of each leaf, and 1 hat. Cut the following shapes for snowman: 2 of each vest shape, 1 flower, 1 leaf, and 1 hat (do not fold felt before cutting out hat).
5. (**Note:** Refer to **Embroidery** instructions, page 158, for embroidery. Use 3 strands of floss unless otherwise indicated. If floss color is not specified, use any color.) Use black floss to work French Knots for eyes and Running Stitch for mouth on snow woman and snowman.
6. Glue noses to faces. Sew 3 buttons along center of snowman.
7. Work Running Stitch along center of each large leaf for snow woman; overlap leaves. Sew a button at overlap.
8. For snow woman's basket, place basket shapes together and work Blanket Stitch along edges of basket. Arrange flowers and small leaves on basket; glue in place. Sew a button to center of each flower.
9. For each side of snowman's vest, place vest shapes together and work Blanket Stitch along edges.
10. For flower on snowman's hat, glue leaf to back of flower. Sew a button to center of flower.

11. Arrange and glue body shapes and hats on 1 corner of afghan.
12. Work Running Stitch close to edges of hats. Use black floss to work Blanket Stitch along edges of body shapes.

13. Glue remaining shapes and Posy and Daisy Ornaments to snow folks and cover-up.
14. Use yarn and large needle to work Blanket Stitch along edges of cover-up.

MINI FELT EVERGREENS (Shown on page 65)

For each tree, you will need assorted colors of felt for posies, black and assorted colors of embroidery floss, gold pearl cotton thread (size 3), clear nylon thread, embroidery needle, assorted buttons, 1"w wooden star cutouts, approx. 7" long twig for trunk, container to hold tree (we used miniature pails and washtubs), floral foam to fill container, sphagnum moss, tracing paper, and a low-temperature glue gun.
For small tree, you will **also** need a 6"h plastic foam cone, a 2³/₄" x 36" strip of green felt, and a Posy Ornament (page 68).
For medium tree, you will **also** need a 9"h plastic foam cone, two 2³/₄" x 36" strips of green felt, and a Daisy Ornament (page 68).
For large tree, you will **also** need a 12"h plastic foam cone, three 2³/₄" x 36" strips of green felt, and a Star Ornament (page 68).

SMALL TREE
1. Place foam in container; glue to secure. Glue sphagnum moss over foam.
2. For trunk, push 1 end of twig into center bottom of plastic foam cone and remaining end into floral foam in container (about 2¹/₂" of twig should show); glue to secure.
3. (**Note:** Refer to **Embroidery** instructions, page 158, for Steps 3 and 4.) Cut scallops along 1 long edge of felt strip. Use 4 strands of black floss to work Blanket Stitch along scalloped edge.
4. To gather long straight edge (top) of strip, use nylon thread to work Running Stitch along edge; knot 1 end. Pull remaining end to loosely gather felt; knot and trim remaining end.
5. Beginning at bottom of cone, wrap felt strip in a spiral around cone, gluing strip in place as you go. At top of cone, form felt into a point and glue in place; if necessary, trim excess felt.
6. Glue ornament to tree for tree topper.

7. For each posy on tree, trace patterns onto tracing paper; cut out. Use patterns to cut shapes from felt. Use 3 strands of floss to work a Cross Stitch, page 158, to secure flower center to flower. Glue leaf to back of flower.
8. For each button with a bow, thread a 10" length of pearl cotton thread through button and tie into a bow at back; trim ends.
9. For each star, glue a button to a wooden star cutout.
10. Glue posies, buttons with bows, stars, and additional buttons to tree.

MEDIUM OR LARGE TREE
Overlap ends of felt strips about 1/2" and glue together to form 1 long strip. To complete tree follow Small Tree instructions.

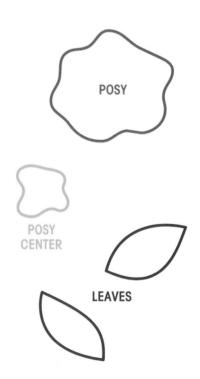

POSY

POSY CENTER

LEAVES

SNOWY DAY VEST (Shown on page 65)

You will need a purchased felt vest (available at fabric and craft stores); felt to line front of vest (we used black); ivory, orange, and assorted colors of felt for appliqués (we used yellow, dark yellow, orange, dark red, green, and dark green); two 1" dia. buttons for vest closure and assorted small white buttons for snow; black and assorted colors of embroidery floss (we used ivory and green); embroidery needle; acetate for template; permanent pen; white chalk pencil; small sharp scissors; tracing paper; transparent tape (if needed); fabric glue; and several Posy Ornaments (page 68).

1. Wash, dry, and press vest and felt according to manufacturer's instructions.
2. For lining pattern, lay vest flat with front facing up. Trace 1 side of vest front onto tracing paper. Draw a second shape about 1" outside traced shape. Cut out pattern along outer line.
3. Use pattern to cut 2 pieces of felt for lining. Set lining pieces aside.
4. For snow woman appliqués, follow Step 1 of Snow Folks instructions, page 71, to enlarge snow woman body, nose, hat, and large leaf patterns. Place body pattern in desired position on vest and trim pattern even with bottom edge of vest; discard bottom of pattern. Use patterns to cut snow woman body shape from ivory felt and nose from orange felt. Cut remaining shapes from other colors of felt.
5. (**Note:** Refer to **Embroidery** instructions, page 158, for embroidery. Use 3 strands of floss unless otherwise indicated. If floss color is not specified, use any color.) Arrange hat and body shape appliqués on vest; glue in place. Use 2 strands of black floss to work Blanket Stitch along edges of body shape. Use 4 strands of black floss to work French Knots for eyes and Running Stitch for mouth.
6. Glue nose to face.
7. Work Running Stitch along centers of leaves. Arrange leaves on snow woman, overlapping ends; sew a button to leaves at overlap.

8. For flower appliqués, arrange Posy Ornaments on vest; glue in place. Stitching through buttonholes, tack ornaments to vest.
9. Sew white buttons to vest for snow.
10. To line each side of vest front, center 1 felt lining shape inside vest front, making sure edges of lining extend evenly beyond edges of vest front; pin in place. Glue lining to vest along shoulder seam and side. Use 6 strands of floss to work Running Stitch along edges of vest front to secure lining. Trim lining extending beyond armholes to desired width.
11. For sawtooth trim, use permanent pen to trace template pattern onto acetate; cut out. Place template at top of untrimmed lining on 1 side of vest front. Use chalk pencil to draw along jagged edge of template. Moving template as necessary, draw around template along untrimmed edges of each vest lining piece. Use small scissors to cut trim along drawn lines.

Fig. 1

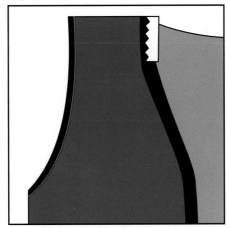

12. For buttonholes, use scissors to cut two 1" slits about 2" apart on right vest front. Work Running Stitch around buttonholes. Mark position of buttonholes on left side of vest and sew 1" dia. buttons to vest at marks.

SWEET FELT STOCKINGS
(Shown on page 66)

For each stocking, you will need one 12" x 21" piece each of black and desired color felt, assorted colors of felt for appliqués (we used ivory, dark yellow, red, dark red, blue, green, dark green, and tan), black and assorted colors of embroidery floss, assorted buttons, embroidery needle, tracing paper, fabric glue, and 1 Daisy Ornament (page 68).

1. Matching dotted lines and aligning arrows, trace stocking pattern onto tracing paper; cut out. Use pattern to cut stocking front from colored felt.
2. For appliqués, trace desired ornament patterns, page 70, onto tracing paper; cut out. Use patterns to cut 1 of each shape from felt (do not fold felt before cutting out cottage). Arrange appliqués and Daisy Ornament on stocking front; glue to secure.
3. (**Note:** Refer to **Embroidery** instructions, page 158, for embroidery. Use 3 strands of floss unless otherwise indicated.) For star appliqué, sew a button to flower center. Work Straight Stitches along center of each leaf. Work Blanket Stitch along edges of star.
4. For cottage appliqué, work Running Stitch close to edges of cottage and chimney. Work straight stitches for windowpanes. Using 6 strands of floss, sew a button to door for doorknob, sew a button to heart, knotting and trimming floss at front of button. For smoke, use 6 strands of floss and take a small stitch at top of chimney. Unthread needle, knot floss, and trim ends about 1 1/2" from chimney.
5. For heart appliqué, work Running Stitch close to edges of ornament front. Use 6 strands of floss to sew buttons to ornament front, knotting and trimming floss at front of buttons.
6. Stitching through buttonholes, tack Daisy Ornament to stocking front.
7. Sew a row of buttons along top of stocking front.
8. Center stocking front on black felt. Work Running Stitch close to side and bottom edges of front. Trim black felt even with top edge of front and about 1" outside side and bottom edges.
9. Follow Step 11 of Snowy Day Vest instructions to cut sawtooth trim along edges of stocking back.
10. For hanger, cut a 1/2" x 4" strip of felt. Fold strip in half to form a loop. Sew ends inside stocking.

TEMPLATE

STOCKING BOTTOM

STOCKING TOP

73

"BEE" MERRY

Our "Bee" Merry collection is full of fresh ideas that will look right at home in a sunroom — or anywhere you'd like a radiant reminder of summer's bounty! The whimsical decorations include a cheery wreath, flowerpot candles, and a tree trimmed with "homegrown" flowers and vegetables. You can even create a farmer's market scene complete with Santa as a jolly old gardener! Instructions for the projects shown here and on the following pages begin on page 78.

A delightful way to continue the gardening theme, a wreath of greenery is adorned with ornaments from the tree, a generous multi-loop bow, and faux vegetables and flowers.

Abuzz with summertime appeal, our **"Bee" Merry Tree** *(page 78)* features giant **Bumblebees** *(page 79)* crafted from paper and wooden cutouts. Hand-colored **Seed-Packet Ornaments** *(page 78)* and **Gardening Gloves** *(page 78)* with colorful fused-on cuffs are tucked among silk flowers, watering cans, and beehives. Lifelike dragonflies can be spied amidst miniature gardening tools, faux vegetables, and bird nests. To complete the outdoor look, pine bark mulch is scattered around the base of the evergreen (shown on page 75).

For **Very Merry Candles** *(page 79)*, clay flowerpots are filled with wax and dressed up with fabric strips and other trims. Arranged together on a weathered bench or displayed separately, these cute candles will add a lighthearted touch to the holiday decor.

Dressed in gardening attire, our **Green Thumb Santa** *(page 79)* is a winsome sight, especially when posed among baskets of garden goodies.

"BEE" MERRY TREE

(Shown on page 75)

It's always springtime in Santa's magical garden, as this unique 6½-foot-tall tree shows. To decorate the whimsical evergreen, Santa has chosen only the best from his vegetable and flower gardens. Cauliflowers, lettuce heads glued into tiny flowerpots, pea pods, melons, radishes tied into bunches with black and white wired ribbon bows, and charming silk flowers are among the harvest on the tree.

For a clever ornament, Santa painted the wooden handles of mini garden tools to resemble carrots and glued various lengths of green chenille stems to the handles for leaves. A raffia bow finishes each one. His Gardening Gloves and Seed-Packet Ornaments (this page) are also easy-to-make ornaments. Small watering cans, eye-catching bird nests with tiny eggs, miniature straw beehives, fanciful Bumblebees (page 79), and appealing dragonflies hovering around the tree all add to the wonderment.

Instead of a conventional tree skirt, Santa has spread pine bark mulch around the base of the tree. Large flowerpots filled with flowers and small trees, small trees in burlap bags, baskets of vegetables, and a large galvanized watering can complete the memorable tree.

GARDENING GLOVES (Shown on page 76)

For each glove, you will need a cotton gardening glove, 2 fabrics for cuff, fusible web, yellow and black acrylic paint, paintbrushes, black felt-tip pen, 10" of white paper wire, tracing paper, and graphite transfer paper.

1. For cuff, measure around ribbing on glove; add ½". Cut a strip of fabric 4" wide by the determined measurement. Match wrong sides and long edges and press fabric strip in half. Cut a ½"w strip from remaining fabric same length as first fabric strip.

2. Fuse web to 1 side of folded fabric strip and to wrong side of narrow strip. Fuse narrow strip along raw edges of folded strip.
3. Overlapping ends at back, fuse strip over ribbing on glove.
4. Trace pattern onto tracing paper. Use transfer paper to transfer pattern to glove.
5. Paint bees black and yellow. Use pen to draw over transferred lines.
6. For hanger, glue ends of paper wire in cuff.

SEED-PACKET ORNAMENTS (Shown on page 76)

For each ornament, you will need a 3" x 4" wooden rectangle cutout, photocopy of seed-packet design, colored pencils, spray adhesive, 2 small buttons, 7" of jute twine for hanger, and a glue gun.

1. Use pencils to color photocopy. Cutting close to design, cut design from paper.
2. Use spray adhesive to glue design to wooden cutout.
3. For hanger, glue ends of twine to top corners of cutout; glue buttons over ends of twine.

BUMBLEBEES

(Shown on page 76)

For each bee, you will need an approx. 4"h wooden heart cutout, yellow paper, black chenille stem, large black button, black felt-tip pen, tracing paper, 6" of floral wire for hanger, and a glue gun.

1. For bee body, trace oval pattern onto tracing paper; cut out. Use pattern to cut body from yellow paper.
2. Use pen to draw approx. ¼"w stripes about ¼" apart on body.
3. For wings, use pen to draw a curved dashed line along center of wooden heart.
4. For head, cut an 8" length from chenille stem. Bend stem in half at center and curl ends. Glue center of stem to back of button.
5. Glue body and head to wings.
6. For hanger, glue center of wire length to back of bee.

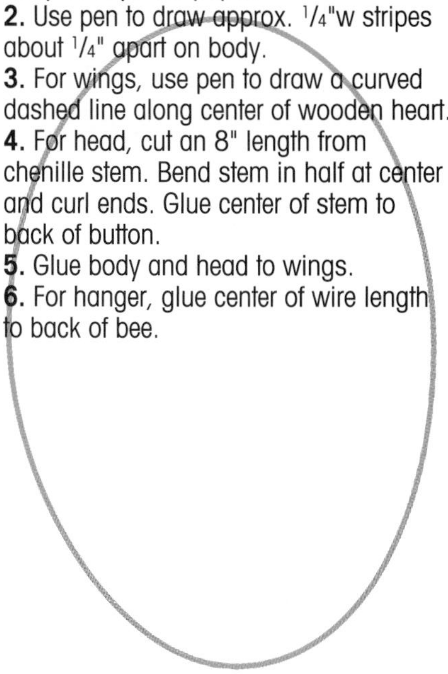

GREEN THUMB SANTA (Shown on page 77)

You will need a pair of infant's overalls and a flannel shirt (we used size 3 - 6 months), a pair of children's boots (we used size 3), 2 pairs of children's white tube socks (we used size 6½ - 11), white thread, red bandanna, 25" muslin square, cotton batting, polyester fiberfill, one 5" dia. and one 7" dia. plastic foam ball, craft mop head, 10" dia. straw doll hat, 3¼"w doll glasses, silk flowers and leaves, jute rope, black felt-tip pen, red colored pencil, 1 large red shank button for nose, straight pins, floral wire, wire cutters, tracing paper, graphite transfer paper, safety pins, and a glue gun.

Note: The Green Thumb Santa is not a toy and should be used for decorative purposes only.

1. Use fiberfill to firmly stuff socks. Sew tops of socks closed. Place large foam ball into shirt for body and use fiberfill to stuff shoulders. Button shirt and place in overalls. With toes of socks as Santa's hands and feet, insert stuffed socks in sleeves of shirt and legs of overalls; use safety pins to secure. If desired, stuff shirt and overalls with more fiberfill to achieve desired results. Fasten overall suspenders. Place boots on feet.

2. Measure around waist of overalls; add 14". Cut a piece of rope the determined measurement. Knot rope around waist of overalls, using belt loops if provided.
3. For head, cover remaining foam ball with cotton batting; smooth in place. Wrap muslin around foam ball, pulling fabric taut and smoothing in place. Pin muslin to ball. Gather excess muslin and wrap tightly with wire (gathered muslin is bottom of head).
4. For eyes, trace pattern onto tracing paper. Use transfer paper to transfer eyes to head. Use black pen to color eyes. Use red pencil to color cheeks.
5. For mustache, cut about eighteen 7" lengths from craft mop. Use floral wire to tightly wrap center of strings. Glue strings to head (gluing each string in place gives best results). Glue red button to mustache for nose.
6. For eyebrows, cut two 1" lengths from mop strings; glue in place.
7. To attach head to body, glue head inside neck of shirt, stuffing excess muslin into shirt. Knot bandanna around neck. Tuck flowers behind bandanna.
8. Place hat and glasses on Santa; if desired, glue to secure.

 EYES

VERY MERRY CANDLES (Shown on page 77)

You will need a 25-pound block of wax (available at craft stores), large coffee can for melting wax, a pan to hold can (an electric frying pan works well), 1 wick weight for each candle, matte Modge Podge® sealer, foam brush, 3 new pencils, newspaper, and duct tape.
For large flowerpot with bumblebee, you will **also** need a 6½" dia. clay flowerpot with saucer, 12" of wire wick (#w-3), photocopy of seed-packet design (page 78), colored pencils, 4 small buttons, natural raffia, silk flowers and leaves, glue gun, and 1 Bumblebee (this page).
For large flowerpot with peas, you will **also** need a 6½" dia. clay flowerpot with saucer, 12" of wire wick (#w-3), a 1¼" x 21" fabric strip, 21" each of ½"w and ¼"w satin ribbon, silk pea pods and flowers, natural raffia, and a glue gun.
For small flowerpot, you will **also** need a 4½" dia. clay flowerpot with saucer, 8" of wire wick (#w-2), a ⅞" x 15" fabric strip for pot, and a ½" x 15" fabric strip for saucer.

Caution: Do not melt wax over an open flame or directly on burner. Do not leave burning candles unattended.

LARGE FLOWERPOTS

1. To prepare flowerpot, place duct tape over hole in bottom of pot. Tie 1 end of wick to wick weight. Secure wick weight in center bottom of pot with duct tape. Pull wick straight up and wind top around pencil. Rest pencil across top of pot.
2. Cover work area with newspaper. Break wax block into small pieces. Place wax pieces in can. Place can in pan and fill pan half full with water. Heat water until wax melts.
3. Pour wax into pot until pot is about ⅔ full. Let wax cool and set for 24 hours.
4. Repeat Steps 2 and 3 twice more, filling pot to bottom of rim on second day and almost to top of rim on third day. (This filling and cooling process allows candle to have a smooth top.)
5. Remove pencil and trim wick.
6. For large flowerpot with bumblebee, invert saucer on top of pot. Knot several

lengths of raffia around pot; trim ends. Glue bee and flowers to knot. Use colored pencils to color photocopy; cut out. Use foam brush to apply sealer to back of colored design. Center design on flowerpot and use brush to smooth in place. Glue buttons to corners.
7. For large flowerpot with peas, use foam brush to apply sealer to wrong side of fabric strip. Wrap strip around rim of pot and smooth in place. Knot several lengths of raffia around rim; trim ends. Glue flowers and pea pods to knot. For saucer, apply sealer to 1 side of each ribbon length and wrap around rim of saucer; smooth in place.

SMALL FLOWERPOT

1. Follow Steps 1 - 5 of Large Flowerpots instructions to make candle.
2. For fabric strips on rim of pot and saucer, use foam brush to apply sealer to wrong sides of fabric strips. Wrap strips around rim of pot and saucer and smooth in place.

A BROWN BAG NOEL

A lighthearted, feel-good Christmas is in the bag with this collection of natural charmers! Fashioned from plain brown paper sacks, the playful trimmings include lots of traditional Yuletide favorites, from country angels to colorful candy canes. Raffia straw, folksy fabrics, a variety of buttons, and jumbo jingle bells add to the decorations' endearing appeal. A cheery sight, the evergreen is laden with paper bows, fabric-wrapped balls, stuffed penny sacks, and padded paper ornaments. To continue the captivating theme, you'll discover a homey wreath, a mantel swag, and a coordinating banner. Glad tidings are easy to spread with special treats from our sweet favor basket or with gifts presented in simple embellished totes. Instructions for the projects shown here and on the following pages begin on page 86.

To create our **"Bag-abond" Confetti Wreath** *(page 89)*, layered fabric and brown paper squares are pinned to a straw wreath. Giant jingle bells and a coordinating bow accent the quaint Christmas decoration.

Christmas wishes are sure to come true with our whimsical **Brown Bag Noel Tree** *(page 86)*. Sitting atop the merrily decorated evergreen is an enchanting **Starburst Tree Topper** *(page 89)*. The branches are brimming with **Brown Bag Ornaments** *(page 86)*, stuffed paper shapes decorated with fused-on fabric Santas, mittens, candy canes, angels, and snowmen. **Jingle Bell Bows** *(page 88)*, **Fabric-Wrapped Christmas Balls** *(page 88)*, a fabric-strip garland, and raffia-tied penny bags also adorn the tree. *(Opposite, top)* To dress up your mantel, a coordinating swag is made from lengths of raffia embellished with paper bows, torn fabric strips, and paper bag tree-trimmers. *(Opposite, bottom)* Large grocery sacks with fused-on fabric trim and raffia bows encircle the base of the evergreen.

For captivating presentations, try our **Decorated Gift Bags and Tags** *(page 91)*. Various sizes of brown paper sacks are embellished with Yuletide motifs from the tree, and paper-scrap cutouts make cheery coordinating tags. *(Opposite)* Brown paper, fabric scraps, and fusible web are used to create this simple **Homespun Wall Hanging** *(page 90)*. Images from the ornament collection give it a timeless touch. Keep a **Basket of Favors** *(page 90)* ready for holiday visitors. A market basket lined with fabric and trimmed with pinked paper strips is loaded with goodie-filled penny sacks and paper mittens.

84

A BROWN BAG NOEL TREE
(Shown on page 81)

Host a country Christmas party and gather friends and family around this 8-foot-tall pine tree. Everyone can help craft the charming decorations using folksy fabrics and brown paper bags.

To trim the homespun tree, begin with a simple jute braid and wind it among the branches. For a quaint garland, gather 1³/₄"w pinked fabric strips along the centers by zigzag stitching over cotton string, then pulling the string to create a ruffled look. Red silk berry stems tucked among the boughs provide a natural backdrop.

The Brown Bag Ornaments (this page), made from fabric-appliquéd brown paper, are fanciful adornments on the evergreen. You'll find plump Santas with fleecy beards, accompanied by snowmen sporting wintry outfits and country angels holding wooden stars. Ribbon-trimmed candy canes and large mittens are cozy companions to the puffy characters. Each mitten is filled with goodies and hung by a paper wire handle. Give guests the mittens or candy-filled penny sacks tied with raffia bows right from the tree, or present the treats from your Basket of Favors (page 90). Also scattered about the tree are Jingle Bell Bows (page 88), made from brown paper and jingle bells, and Fabric-Wrapped Christmas Balls (page 88).

Topping the evergreen is our Starburst Tree Topper (page 89), a prairie-picked bouquet of wooden stars and buttons in a sack of "wishes." At the tree base, a brown bag tree ring is a clever alternative to a traditional tree skirt. The bags double as unique gift packaging, too. To make each one, simply fuse fabric to the printed side of a grocery bag. Place gift in bag; fold top of bag down and staple in place. Glue a wispy raffia bow over the staple for a rustic country touch.

BROWN BAG ORNAMENTS (Shown on page 82)

For each ornament, you will need two 8¹/₂" squares of brown paper (see Brown Bag Basics, page 91), fabrics for appliqués, fusible web, lightweight interfacing (if needed), polyester fiberfill, assorted buttons, black felt-tip pen, serrated-cut craft scissors, craft glue, and a glue gun.

For angel, you will **also** need cosmetic blush, red curly wool doll hair, a 2"w wooden star cutout, an approx. 4" long ¹/₈" dia. twig, and natural raffia.

For candy cane, you will **also** need 10¹/₂" of ³/₈"w red grosgrain ribbon for stripes, ³/₈"w fusible web tape, natural raffia, and aluminum foil.

For mitten, you will **also** need natural paper wire; natural raffia; 5" of berry stem; and wrapped candy, candy sticks, and candy canes.

For snowman, you will **also** need a 2¹/₄" length of jute twine and a silk berry stem.

For Santa, you will **also** need cotton batting for beard and hat trim.

ANGEL
1. (**Note:** Use hot glue unless otherwise indicated.) Use angel patterns and follow **Making Appliqués,** page 158.
2. Arrange appliqués at center of 1 brown paper square; fuse in place.
3. Use pen to draw stitches around angel.
4. Use pen to draw dots for eyes and detail lines on dress and legs. Use fingertip to apply blush to cheeks.
5. Place paper squares wrong sides together and cut out angel about ¹/₂" outside drawn stitches.
6. Use craft glue to glue edges of angel together, leaving a small opening for stuffing. Stuff ornament with fiberfill; glue opening closed. Use craft scissors to trim edges of ornament.
7. For hair, cut a 5¹/₂" length of doll hair. Arrange hair around top of head; glue to secure.
8. For star wand, glue star cutout to 1 end of twig. Tie several lengths of raffia into a bow; glue bow to remaining end of twig. Glue wand to 1 angel hand.
9. Glue buttons to dress, shoes, and star.
10. For wings, tie several lengths of raffia into an 8"w bow; trim streamers close to bow. Glue bow to center back of angel.

CANDY CANE
1. Use candy cane pattern and follow **Making Appliqués,** page 158.
2. For stripes on candy cane, fuse web tape to 1 side of ribbon length. Cut ribbon into seven 1¹/₂" lengths. Place a piece of foil shiny side up on ironing board. Place candy cane appliqué on foil. Spacing evenly, arrange ribbon lengths on appliqué; fuse in place. Remove appliqué from foil and trim ribbon ends even with edges of appliqué.
3. Fuse appliqué to center of 1 brown paper square.
4. To assemble candy cane, follow Steps 3, 5, and 6 of Angel instructions.
5. Tie several lengths of raffia into a bow. Hot glue bow and a button to candy cane.

MITTEN
1. Use mitten and heart patterns, page 87, and follow Steps 1 - 3 of Angel instructions.
2. Use pen to draw stitches over edges of heart appliqué.
3. To assemble mitten, follow Step 5 of Angel Ornament instructions. Leaving top edge open, use craft glue to glue edges of mitten together. Use craft scissors to trim edges of ornament. Stuff mitten with a small amount of fiberfill.
4. For handle, cut an 18" length of paper wire. Loop wire and glue ends inside mitten.
5. Tie several lengths of raffia into a bow and glue to mitten. Glue buttons to mitten and bow. Glue 1 end of berry stem into mitten.
6. Place candy in mitten.

SNOWMAN
1. Use snowman patterns, page 87, and follow Steps 1 - 3 of Angel instructions.
2. Use pen to draw dots for eyes and mouth.
3. To assemble ornament, follow Steps 5 and 6 of Angel instructions.
4. For scarf ends, cut a ³/₄" x 5¹/₄" fabric strip; fringe ends and knot at center. Glue knot to 1 side of scarf appliqué.
5. Glue twine length to hat for band. Cut leaves and berries from berry stem and glue to 1 side of hat.
6. Glue 2 buttons to center front of snowman.

CANDY CANE

ANGEL

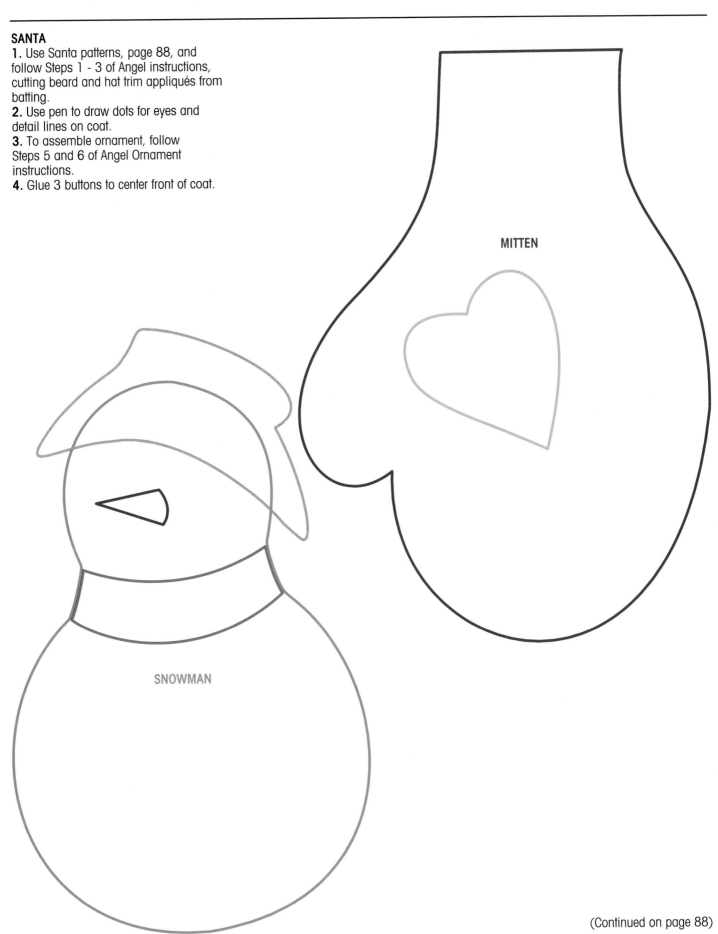

SANTA

1. Use Santa patterns, page 88, and follow Steps 1 - 3 of Angel instructions, cutting beard and hat trim appliqués from batting.

2. Use pen to draw dots for eyes and detail lines on coat.

3. To assemble ornament, follow Steps 5 and 6 of Angel Ornament instructions.

4. Glue 3 buttons to center front of coat.

MITTEN

SNOWMAN

(Continued on page 88)

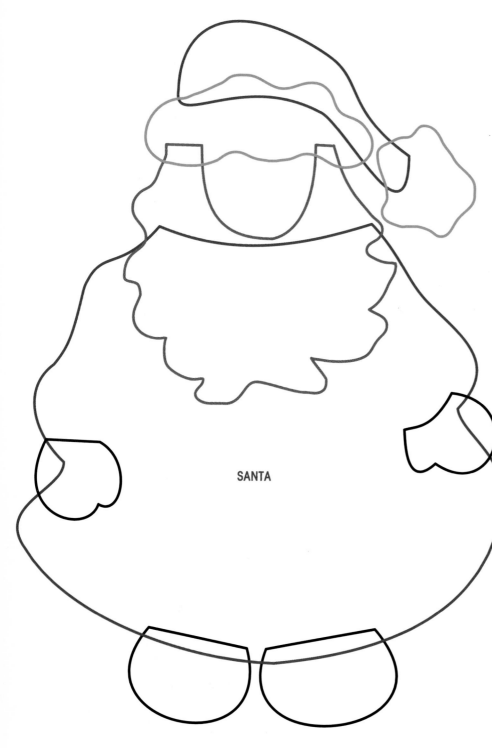

SANTA

JINGLE BELL BOWS
(Shown on page 82)

For each bow, you will need one
2" x 14½" and two 2" x 7" strips of
brown paper (see Brown Bag Basics,
page 91), large jingle bell, floral wire,
wire cutters, and a glue gun.

1. For bow, overlap ends of long paper
strip about ½" to form a loop; glue ends
together. Flatten loop with overlap at
center back. Pinch loop at center to
gather.
2. For each streamer, pinch 1 end of
1 short paper strip. Glue pinched end to
center back of bow and trim remaining
end. Bend streamers as desired.
3. Thread a length of wire through hanger
on jingle bell. Wrap ends of wire around
center of bow to back; twist ends tightly
to secure and bend into a hook for
hanger.

FABRIC-WRAPPED CHRISTMAS BALLS
(Shown on page 82)

For each ball, you will need a 3" dia.
plastic foam ball, a 12" fabric square,
button, natural raffia, floral wire, wire
cutters, and a glue gun.

1. Place fabric square wrong side up.
Place ball at center and gather edges of
fabric at top of ball. Tightly wrap a length
of wire around gathers to secure; trim
wire ends.
2. Trim fabric edges even about 1¼"
from ball. Wrap several lengths of raffia
around gathered fabric to cover wire and
knot raffia to secure. Glue button to knot.
3. For hanger, cut a 6½" length of raffia.
Knot ends together and glue knot into top
of ornament.

STARBURST TREE TOPPER (Shown on page 82)

You will need a small brown grocery bag and brown paper (see Brown Bag Basics, page 91), white paper, fabric, fusible web, assorted buttons, six 2"w wooden star cutouts, nine 10" to 16" long twigs (about 1/8" dia.), floral foam brick to fit in bottom of bag, natural raffia, black felt-tip pen, serrated-cut craft scissors, tracing paper, graphite transfer paper, and a glue gun.

1. Fuse web to brown paper, white paper, and wrong side of fabric.

2. For label on bag, use craft scissors to cut a 3⁵/₈" x 6" piece of brown paper. Trace pattern onto tracing paper. Use transfer paper to transfer pattern to brown paper piece. Use pen to draw over words and stitches.

3. Cut a 4" x 6¹/₂" piece of white paper and a 5" x 7" piece of fabric.

4. Center and fuse fabric piece to front of bag about 1" from bottom. Center and fuse white paper piece, then brown paper piece to fabric piece.

5. Use pen to draw stitches over edges of fabric piece.

6. For starburst, place foam brick in bag. Glue buttons to stars. Glue stars and additional buttons to ends of twigs. Insert twigs into foam brick, arranging as desired.

7. Tie several lengths of raffia into a bow around top of bag.

"BAG-ABOND" CONFETTI WREATH (Shown on page 80)

You will need a 14¹/₂" dia. straw wreath; brown paper (see Brown Bag Basics, page 91) and assorted fabrics to cover wreath; a 6" x 1²/₃ yd fabric strip for bow; fusible web; seven large jingle bells; greening pins; floral wire; glue gun; and a rotary cutter, cutting mat, and ruler (optional).

1. For hanger on wreath, bend an 18" length of floral wire in half. Twist wire together about 2" from bend to form a loop. Keeping loop at back of wreath, wrap wire ends around wreath and twist together to secure.

2. (**Note:** If you cut squares for Step 2, we recommend using a rotary cutter.) Tear or cut desired number of approx. 3" squares from brown paper and fabrics to cover wreath (we tore about 180 paper squares and 90 fabric squares).

3. Place 1 fabric square right side up between 2 paper squares. Insert greening pin through center of layered squares, then into wreath. Repeat with remaining squares, pinning squares close together and folding edges away from wreath to create fullness and cover wreath.

4. For bow, cut a 3" x 1²/₃ yd strip of web (use several pieces if necessary). Fuse

web strip along 1 long edge on wrong side of fabric strip. Matching long edges, fuse fabric strip in half. Trim fabric strip to 2³/₄"w. Cut a 6" length from end of strip and set aside for bow center. Form long fabric strip into a double-loop bow with approx. 8" streamers; wrap center of bow with wire to secure.

5. For bow center, wrap short fabric strip around center of bow, covering wire and overlapping ends at back; glue to secure.

6. Glue jingle bells and bow to wreath.

HOMESPUN WALL HANGING (Shown on page 85)

You will need a 23" x 24" piece of heavy poster board, a 25" x 26" fabric piece for background, fabrics for appliqués and hanging loops, fusible web, lightweight fusible interfacing (if needed), four 8½" x 9" pieces of brown paper (see Brown Bag Basics, page 91), red curly wool doll hair, cosmetic blush, an approx. 2"w wooden star cutout, a 3½" long ⅛" dia. twig, cotton batting for Santa beard and hat trim, 2" of jute twine, assorted buttons, silk berry stem, natural raffia, 26½" of ⅜" dia. wooden dowel, 2 natural wooden beads to fit over ends of dowel, black felt-tip pen, and a glue gun.

1. Fuse web to wrong side of background fabric and brown paper pieces.
2. Center and fuse fabric piece to poster board; wrap excess fabric over edges and fuse to back.
3. For corner block appliqués, use square pattern and follow **Making Appliqués**, page 158, to make 9 squares.

4. Arrange paper pieces and fabric squares on background; fuse in place.
5. Use pen and a ruler to draw stitches close to edges of each paper piece. Glue a button to each corner block.
6. For angel, tie several lengths of raffia into a 7"w bow; trim streamers close to bow. Center and glue bow about 2¾" from top of 1 paper piece.
7. To assemble angel on paper piece over raffia bow, follow Steps 1 - 9 (omitting Steps 5 and 6) of Angel instructions, Brown Bag Ornaments, page 86.
8. To assemble snowman on another paper piece, follow Steps 1 - 6 (omitting Step 3) of Snowman instructions, Brown Bag Ornaments, page 86.
9. To assemble Santa on another piece, follow Steps 1 - 4 (omitting Step 3) of Santa instructions, Brown Bag Ornaments, page 87. Tie several lengths of raffia into a small bow and glue bow to

Santa. Cut a small piece from berry stem and glue to bow.
10. To assemble mitten on remaining paper piece, follow Steps 1 and 2 of Mitten instructions, Brown Bag Ornaments, page 86. Tie several lengths of raffia into a bow. Glue bow to mitten. Cut a piece from berry stem and glue to mitten. Glue buttons to mitten and bow.
11. For hanging loops, cut three 4" x 5¼" pieces of fabric. Fuse web to wrong side of each piece. Press long edges to center and fuse in place.
12. Matching ends, fold each fabric strip in half to form a loop. Extending loops about 1½" beyond each corner block appliqué at top of wall hanging, glue ends of fabric strips to back of wall hanging.
13. Insert dowel through hanging loops and glue a bead to each end.

SQUARE

BASKET OF FAVORS (Shown on page 85)

You will need a chipwood market basket with handle (we used an 8½" x 14½" basket); fabrics for basket trim and mitten appliqués; fabric piece cut with pinking shears to line basket; fusible web; polyester fiberfill; brown paper (see Brown Bag Basics, page 91); penny sacks; assorted buttons; black felt-tip pen; natural raffia; silk berry stem; wrapped candy, candy sticks, and candy canes; serrated-cut craft scissors; craft glue; glue gun; and several Mittens, Brown Bag Ornaments (page 86).

1. (**Note:** Use hot glue unless otherwise indicated.) For basket trim, use craft scissors to cut paper into strips about half as wide as wooden strips of basket. Use pen and a ruler to draw stitches along center of each strip. Placing paper strips at centers of wooden strips of basket, weave paper strips through basket. If necessary, glue strips to basket to secure.
2. Fuse web to basket trim fabrics. Cut strips from fabrics to fit on basket rim and handle; fuse strips to basket.
3. Glue berry stem to 1 side of handle.
4. Line basket with fabric and set aside.
5. (**Note:** For each medium or small mitten, follow Steps 5 - 8.) Cut two 7" squares of brown paper. Use either medium mitten pattern or small mitten and square patterns and follow **Making Appliqués**, page 158.

6. Center and fuse appliqué(s) to 1 paper square.
7. Use pen to draw stitches around mitten and over edges of square on small mitten. Glue buttons to mittens.
8. Place paper squares wrong sides together and use craft scissors to cut out mitten about ½" outside drawn stitches. Leaving top edge open, use craft glue to glue edges of mitten together.
9. For each medium mitten, tie several lengths of raffia into a bow and glue to mitten. Glue button to bow.
10. For each penny sack, place candy in sack and tie several lengths of raffia into a bow around top.
11. Place mittens, penny sacks, and Mitten ornaments in basket.

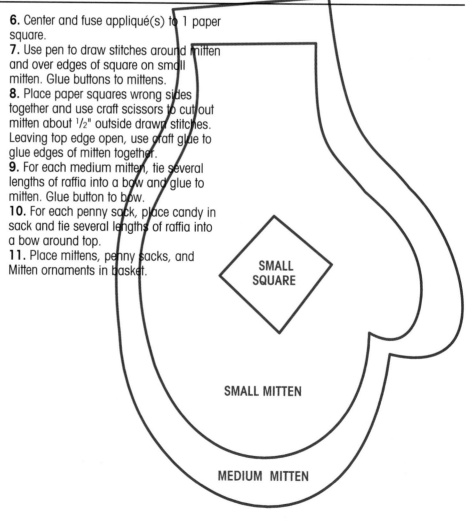

SMALL SQUARE

SMALL MITTEN

MEDIUM MITTEN

90

DECORATED GIFT BAGS AND TAGS (Shown on page 84)

For each bag, you will need fabrics for appliqués, fusible web, lightweight fusible interfacing (if needed), assorted buttons, black felt-tip pen, and a glue gun.

For Santa bag, you will **also** need an 8" x 10" brown gift bag with handles, cotton batting for beard and hat trim, large jingle bell, silk berry stem, natural raffia, and tissue paper to line bag.

For snowman bag, you will **also** need a brown lunch bag, white acrylic paint, a small household paintbrush, silk berry stem, 2¹/₄" length of jute twine, newspaper, and tissue paper to line bag.

For rustic labeled bag, you will **also** need a brown lunch bag, heavy brown paper (see Brown Bag Basics, this page), tan paper, white acrylic paint, small household paintbrush, natural raffia, newspaper, serrated-cut craft scissors, and a stapler.

For each wee parcel sack, you will **also** need a penny sack, fabric to cover sack, natural raffia, hole punch, and serrated-cut craft scissors.

For each gift tag, you will **also** need heavy brown paper (see Brown Bag Basics, this page), silk berry stem and natural raffia for berry decorated tag, and serrated-cut craft scissors.

SANTA BAG
1. Follow Steps 1 - 4 (omitting Step 3) of Santa instructions, Brown Bag Ornaments, page 87, to fuse appliqués to front of bag.
2. Tie several lengths of raffia into a bow.
3. Thread several lengths of raffia through hanger of jingle bell. Keeping bell at front, knot raffia around center of bow and handle of bag; trim ends.
4. Cut two lengths from berry stem and glue to bag below bow.
5. Line bag with tissue paper.

SNOWMAN BAG
1. Cover work surface with newspaper. To spatter-paint bag, dip paintbrush into diluted white paint. Hold paintbrush over scrap paper and tap handle once to remove excess paint. Tap paintbrush over bag as desired.
2. Follow Steps 1 - 6 (omitting Step 3 and drawing stitches around snowman) of Snowman instructions, Brown Bag Ornaments, page 86, to fuse appliqués to front of bag.
3. For cuff, fold top of bag down about 1¹/₄". Use pen to draw stitches close to top of cuff.
4. Line bag with tissue paper.

RUSTIC LABELED BAG
1. Follow Step 1 of Snowman Bag instructions to spatter-paint front of bag.
2. Place gift in bag. Fold top of bag about 2¹/₄" to front for flap. Staple flap closed at center.
3. For tag, fuse web to wrong sides of fabric and brown paper.
4. Cut a 2³/₈" x 3³/₈" piece of fabric, a 3¹/₄" x 4¹/₄" piece of tan paper, and a 1¹/₄" x 2¹/₄" piece of brown paper. Use craft scissors to cut an additional 3" x 4" piece of brown paper.
5. Center and fuse large brown paper piece, fabric piece, and small brown paper piece to tan paper piece.
6. Use pen to write name and draw stitches over edges of fabric piece and small brown paper piece.
7. Thread several lengths of raffia through a button and tie into a bow at front. Glue button to tag. Glue tag to bag.

WEE PARCEL SACKS
1. For each sack, fuse web to wrong side of fabric.
2. Cut a piece of fabric same size as front of sack and fuse to front of sack.
3. For heart appliqué, use heart pattern and follow **Making Appliqués**, page 158.
4. Fuse heart to sack. Glue buttons to sack.
5. Place gift in sack. Fold top of sack about 1" to front for flap. Use craft scissors to trim edges of flap.
6. Use pen to draw stitches along edges of flap and over edges of heart.
7. Punch 2 holes close together at center of flap. Thread several lengths of raffia through holes and tie into a bow at front.

GIFT TAGS
1. For mitten tag, trace mitten tag pattern onto tracing paper; cut out. Use craft scissors and pattern to cut mitten from heavy brown paper.
2. For rectangle tag, use craft scissors to cut a 3" x 4" rectangle from heavy brown paper.
3. For heart-appliquéd tag, use heart pattern and follow **Making Appliqués**, page 158. Fuse heart to desired tag shape. Use pen to draw stitches over edges of heart.
4. For berry-decorated tag, tie several lengths of raffia into a small bow. Glue bow to tag. Glue button to bow and a short length of berry stem above bow.
5. If desired, use pen to draw stitches close to edges of tag and to write greeting on tag.

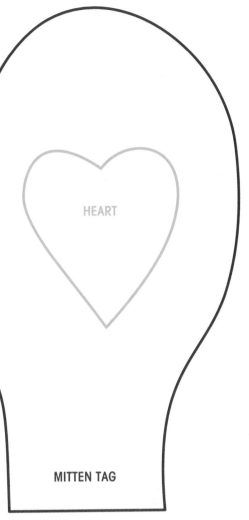

HEART

MITTEN TAG

BROWN BAG BASICS

Most of the projects in this section are made using brown paper recycled from grocery bags.

To prepare paper, cut grocery bag from top to bottom along one corner, then cut bottom from bag and discard. Lay paper printed side down on a protected surface and use a dry iron on cotton setting to press paper flat. Treat printed side of paper as the wrong side.

For heavy brown paper, use web to fuse two same-size pieces of paper wrong sides together, then cut desired size piece or shape from paper.

To decorate bags, place flattened bag with side to be embellished up, unless otherwise indicated. When covering bag with fabric, apply fabric to printed side of bag.

THE SHARING OF CHRISTMAS

One of the greatest joys of the holiday season is seeing the delight that a handmade gift brings to a friend or loved one. Our wonderful collection of wintry wearables provides plenty of ways to brighten someone's Christmas. You'll discover festive clothing for everyone: For Mom, there's a sweet sweater with stenciled bows and holly, and for Dad, a T-shirt decorated with the jolly old elf dressed as a football player. A whimsical painted candyland scene embellishes a dress that's sure to tickle a little girl's fancy, and a Santa bear appliqué adorns a little boy's shirt. Spreading Yuletide cheer has never been easier than with these terrific gifts created and given with love!

$\mathcal{Y}$our favorite little fellow will look "beary" handsome in this **Santa Bear T-shirt** (page 104) featuring machine appliquéd cutouts. (Opposite) Christmas appliqués give country appeal to our charming **Santa Patch-Pocket Thermal Dress** (page 102) and **Angel-Bordered Thermal Dress** (page 103)! To create these Yuletide fashions, skirts made of folksy fabrics are simply sewn to cropped thermal shirts.

*T*his gridiron-inspired shirt will be a favorite of football fanatics. The **Santa Bowl Shirt** (page 106) is a cinch to make using paints and fusible letters.

A child with the gift of gab will love this cute **"Dial 1-800-Santa" Cardigan** (page 108). *The painted jacket shows Santa taking a call from one of his many admirers.*

A buzz with charm, our *"bee-utiful"* **Santa's Garden Wreath Sweatshirt** (page 110) *is sure to delight a gardening enthusiast. The design is simply transferred and painted on a purchased sweatshirt.*

*O*ur **Sugarplum Fantasy Dress** *(page 106) will enchant a youngster. Adorned with stenciled motifs, rickrack, and a cheery polka-dot bow, a plain denim dress becomes a little girl's dream.*

*J*ust for baby, our **Jolly Santa Sweatshirt** *(page 110) is decorated with a quick-to-finish cross stitch motif.*

*W*rap up a happy holiday with this **Ribbons and Holly**
Stenciled Sweater (page 103). Clear glass beads add a sparkling touch.

*T*he holidays will shine with our **Starry Shirt** (page 102). A plain top is "strung" with button-embellished fabric cutouts and "embossed" star motifs for a festive finish.

*D*ressed in brilliant blue, a happy-go-lucky snowman is cross stitched on a ready-made vest for fun fashionwear. The **Frosty Fellow Stitched Vest** (page 105) is also enhanced with perky plaid lapels, embroidered snowflakes, and simple fabric appliqués.

*The angelic little redhead on this top will steal your heart away! Heavenly appliqués, easy pen "stitching," and buttons adorn our whimsical **Country Angel Cardigan** (page 105).*

STARRY SHIRT (Shown on page 100)

You will need an ecru long-sleeve T-shirt, fabrics for appliqués, fusible web, lightweight fusible interfacing (if needed), low-loft polyester bonded batting, stabilizer, thread and yarn to match shirt, clear nylon thread, assorted buttons, black embroidery floss, permanent felt-tip pen, tracing paper, a large needle, and fabric glue.

1. Wash, dry, and press shirt and fabrics.
2. (**Note:** For each padded star, follow Steps 2 - 5.) Use pen to trace blue and large red star patterns together on a square of tracing paper. Pin pattern to shirt. Cut one 6" square each of muslin and batting. Place batting, then muslin on wrong side of shirt behind star pattern; pin batting and muslin in place.
3. Use matching thread and machine stitch over red star pattern. Remove pins. On wrong side of shirt, carefully trim batting only close to stitching; repin muslin and pattern in place.
4. Stitch over blue star pattern. Carefully tear pattern away from stitching. On wrong side of shirt, use pinking shears to trim muslin about 1/4" from outer stitching lines and clip corners of muslin.
5. Thread a 2/3 yd length of yarn onto needle. On wrong side of shirt, insert needle through muslin backing at 1 corner of star into channel created by lines of stitching. Leaving enough yarn to knot at end, push needle and yarn along channel to next corner. Pull needle through muslin backing and reinsert it into channel close to previous exit point; push needle to next corner, leaving a small loop of yarn (**Fig. 1**). Continue inserting yarn into channels of star. Knot yarn ends together at starting point and glue to secure.

Fig. 1

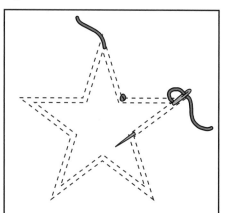

6. For appliqués, use small and large red star patterns and follow **Making Appliqués**, page 158, to make 4 large stars and 2 small stars.
7. Arrange stars on shirt and fuse in place.

8. Use nylon thread and follow **Machine Appliqué**, page 158, to stitch over edges of appliqués.
9. Use 3 strands of black floss and work Running Stitch, page 159, to connect stars on front of shirt.
10. Use floss to sew buttons to stars.

SANTA PATCH-POCKET THERMAL DRESS (Shown on page 94)

You will need a child's ecru thermal shirt (we used a 3T size); fabric for skirt (we used about 3/4 yd of 44/45"w fabric); two 4 7/8" x 6 1/4" fabric pieces for pockets; two 2" x 4 7/8" fabric pieces for pocket facings; peach fabric, red print fabric, and ecru felt for appliqués; fusible web; lightweight fusible interfacing; stabilizer; clear nylon thread and thread to match shirt and fabrics; two 1/2" dia. red buttons; 3/4 yd of 1/8"w green grosgrain ribbon; 1/2 yd of 1/4"w red grosgrain ribbon; red and black embroidery floss; fabric marking pen; black permanent pen; tracing paper; graphite transfer paper; a rotary cutter and cutting mat (optional); and a ruler.

1. Follow Steps 1 - 6 of Angel-Bordered Thermal Dress instructions, page 103, to make dress, reserving bottom of shirt for Santa beard appliqués.
2. (**Note:** Follow Steps 2 - 7 for each pocket.) Fuse interfacing to wrong side of pocket fabric piece.
3. For Santa appliqués, use patterns and follow **Making Appliqués**, page 158, to make face from peach fabric, hat from red print, hat trim and pom-pom from ecru felt, and beard from reserved section of shirt.
4. Arrange appliqués at center of pocket piece with bottom of beard even with 1 short edge (bottom) of pocket piece; fuse in place.

5. Use nylon thread and follow **Machine Appliqué**, page 158, to stitch over raw edges of appliqués.
6. Trace Santa face pattern (shown in grey) onto tracing paper. Use transfer paper to transfer face to Santa. Use black pen to color eyes. Following **Embroidery** instructions, page 158, use 3 strands of red floss to work Running Stitch for cheeks and 4 strands of black floss to work straight stitches for mouth. Sew 1 red button to face for nose.
7. For pocket facing, press 1 long edge (bottom) of 1 pocket facing fabric piece 1/2" to wrong side. Matching top edges of pocket and facing, sew facing to pocket along side and top edges. Clip corners, turn facing to wrong side of pocket, and press. Press side edges of pocket 1/2" to wrong side. Trim bottom edge of pocket even with edge of beard appliqué.
8. To attach pockets to skirt, pin pockets to skirt. With thread to match skirt in bobbin, use nylon thread and a medium width zigzag stitch with a short stitch length to stitch along side and bottom edges of each pocket.
9. Cut a 7" length from green ribbon. Form remaining ribbons into a multi-loop bow; tie short green ribbon length around center to secure. Use a safety pin on inside of dress to pin bow to dress.

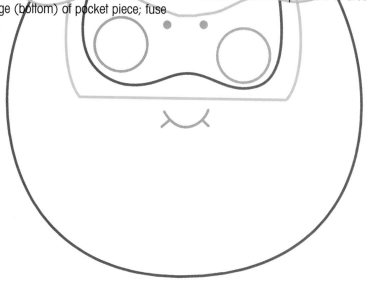

ANGEL-BORDERED THERMAL DRESS (Shown on page 94)

You will need a child's thermal shirt (we used a 5T size), fabric for skirt (we used about 1 yd of 44/45"w fabric), 2 coordinating fabrics for border, a 1³/₄"w x 24" torn fabric strip for bow, fabrics for appliqués, fusible web, lightweight fusible interfacing (if needed), stabilizer, clear nylon thread and thread to match shirt and fabrics, fabric marking pen, a rotary cutter and cutting mat (optional), and a ruler.

1. Wash, dry, and press shirt and fabrics.
2. (**Note:** We recommend using a rotary cutter for cutting shirt, skirt, and border fabrics.) Mark desired placement of top of skirt on shirt with a pin (we placed the top of our skirt about 1¹/₂" below bottom of button placket). Measure from pin to desired skirt length; add 3¹/₂". Measure around bottom edge of shirt; multiply by 1.6. Cut a piece of fabric the determined measurements.

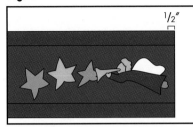

STAR A

3. For bodice, use fabric marking pen and ruler to draw a line across shirt ¹/₂" below pin. Cut off bottom of shirt along drawn line.
4. (**Note:** Unless otherwise indicated, work with fabrics right sides together and use a ¹/₂" seam allowance for sewing steps.) Sew short edges of skirt fabric piece together to form a tube. Press seam allowance open.
5. To gather skirt, baste ¹/₂" and ¹/₄" from 1 raw edge (top) of skirt. Pull basting threads, gathering skirt to fit bottom edge of bodice; knot threads and trim ends. Adjust gathers evenly. With skirt seam at center back and matching raw edges, pin skirt to bodice. Sew skirt to bodice. Press seam allowance toward bodice.

STAR B

6. For hem, press bottom edge of skirt 1" to wrong side; press 2" to wrong side again and blindstitch in place.
7. For border, measure around bottom edge of skirt; add 1". Cut a 6"w strip from 1 border fabric and a 5"w strip from second border fabric the determined measurement (piecing as necessary).
8. Press long edges of narrow border strip ¹/₂" to wrong side. Center narrow strip on wide strip; pin in place. Use matching thread to topstitch along pressed edges of narrow strip.
9. To determine number of angels on border, measure around bottom edge of skirt again; divide measurement by 11 and round down to the nearest whole number.
10. For appliqués on border, use patterns and follow **Making Appliqués**, page 158, to make number of angels determined in

Step 9. Make 1 A star and 2 B stars for each angel. Make 2 additional B stars for bodice.
11. Arrange stars on bodice; fuse in place.
12. For border, start about ¹/₂" from right end and arrange 1 angel, 1 A star, and 2 B stars along center of border (**Fig. 1**). Continue arranging appliqués on border to ¹/₂" from left end. Fuse in place.

Fig. 1

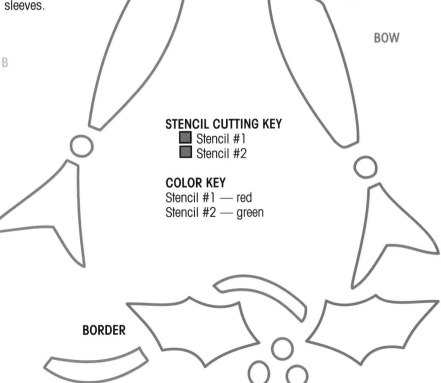

13. Use nylon thread and follow **Machine Appliqué**, page 158, to stitch over edges of appliqués.
14. Matching right sides and ends, fold border in half. Sew ends together to form a tube; press seam allowance open. Press raw edges ¹/₂" to wrong side. Turn right side out.
15. Arrange border on skirt as desired and pin in place. Topstitch border to skirt along outer pressed edges.
16. Tie torn fabric strip into a bow. Use a safety pin on inside of dress to pin bow to dress.

RIBBONS AND HOLLY STENCILED SWEATER (Shown on page 99)

You will need a women's white cotton knit sweater (we used a medium size), red and green fabric paint, acetate for stencils, stencil brushes or small sponge pieces, 5mm green beads (we used Mill Hill™ # 5270 clear glass pebble beads), thread to match sweater, craft knife and cutting mat, paper towels, removable tape (optional), either a T-shirt form or cardboard covered with waxed paper to fit in body of sweater, and 2 cardboard pieces covered with waxed paper to fit in sleeves.

1. Wash, dry, and press sweater. Insert T-shirt form into sweater. Insert cardboard pieces into sleeves.
2. Using bow and border patterns, follow **Stenciling** instructions, page 159, to stencil designs on sweater.
3. Remove T-shirt form and cardboard pieces from sweater.
4. Sew beads to sweater.

BOW

STENCIL CUTTING KEY
■ Stencil #1
■ Stencil #2

COLOR KEY
Stencil #1 — red
Stencil #2 — green

BORDER

SANTA BEAR T-SHIRT (Shown on page 95)

You will need a child's long-sleeve shirt (we used a size 5T), fabrics for appliqués, fusible web, lightweight fusible interfacing (if needed), clear nylon thread and thread to match shirt, stabilizer, a $5/8$" dia. white pom-pom, and a black permanent pen.

1. Wash, dry, and press shirt and fabrics.
2. Use patterns and follow **Making Appliqués**, page 158, to make 2 stars and 1 of each remaining shape.
3. Arrange appliqués on shirt and fuse in place.
4. Use nylon thread and follow **Machine Appliqué**, page 158, to stitch over edges of appliqués.
5. Use pen to draw eyes and mouth on face.
6. Sew pom-pom to point of hat.

STAR

COUNTRY ANGEL CARDIGAN (Shown on page 101)

You will need a women's cardigan with pocket, fabrics for appliqués, fusible web, lightweight fusible interfacing (if needed), clear nylon thread and thread to match cardigan, stabilizer, red curly acrylic doll hair, assorted buttons, 5/8" silver bell, 8" of 1/8"w green satin ribbon, red fabric crayon, black permanent pen, tracing paper, graphite transfer paper, and fabric glue.

1. Wash, dry, and press cardigan and fabrics.
2. Use pen to write "I hear an Angel sing" on pocket and "when a bell rings . . ."

along bottom edge of cardigan. Draw stitches along front of cardigan next to buttonholes, bottom edge, sleeve openings, and top of pocket.
3. Use angel patterns, page 86, and wing and star patterns, this page, and follow **Making Appliqués**, page 158, to make angel, 2 wings (1 in reverse), and 7 stars.
4. Arrange wing and angel appliqués on cardigan; fuse in place.
5. For each star appliqué, fuse web to wrong side of desired background fabric. Fuse star to background fabric. Cutting close to star, cut star from background fabric.

6. Arrange stars on cardigan and fuse in place.
7. Use nylon thread and follow **Machine Appliqué**, page 158, to stitch over edges of appliqués.
8. Use pen to draw stitches close to angel, black dots for eyes, and detail lines on dress and legs. Follow crayon manufacturer's instructions to lightly color cheeks red.
9. For hair, cut an approx. 3 1/2" length of doll hair. Glue hair around top of head.
10. Thread ribbon through hanger of bell and tie into a bow. Use a safety pin on inside of cardigan to pin bell to angel.
11. Sew buttons to cardigan.

FROSTY FELLOW STITCHED VEST (Shown on page 100)

You will need a women's ivory canvas vest with lapels (we used a medium size), one 8" x 10" piece each of 8.5-mesh waste canvas and lightweight non-fusible interfacing, embroidery floss to match appliqué fabrics and to stitch design (see Color Key), masking tape, fabrics to cover lapels and for appliqués, fusible web, clear nylon thread and thread to match vest, tracing paper, embroidery hoop (optional), tweezers, and a spray bottle filled with water.

1. Wash, dry, and press vest and fabrics.
2. Follow Working on Waste Canvas, page 158, to stitch design on vest. Use 6 strands of floss for Cross Stitch and 2 for Backstitch except as noted in color key.
3. For lapel pattern, lay vest flat and trace edges of 1 lapel onto tracing paper. Add 1/4" to pattern all around; cut out pattern. Fuse web to wrong side of lapel fabric. Cut 2 lapels from fabric, 1 in reverse. Clipping edges as necessary, press edges of each lapel shape 1/4" to wrong side all around, fusing edges in place. Fuse fabric lapels to lapels on vest. With thread to match vest in bobbin, use nylon thread and a medium width zigzag stitch with a short stitch length to stitch over edges of lapels.
4. For appliqués, use patterns and follow **Making Appliqués**, page 158. Arrange appliqués on vest and fuse in place. Use nylon thread and follow **Machine Appliqué**, page 158, to stitch over edges of appliqués.
5. (**Note:** Refer to **Embroidery** instructions, page 158, for Step 5.) Using 4 strands of floss to match appliqué fabrics, stitch Straight Stitches and French Knots to make snowflakes.

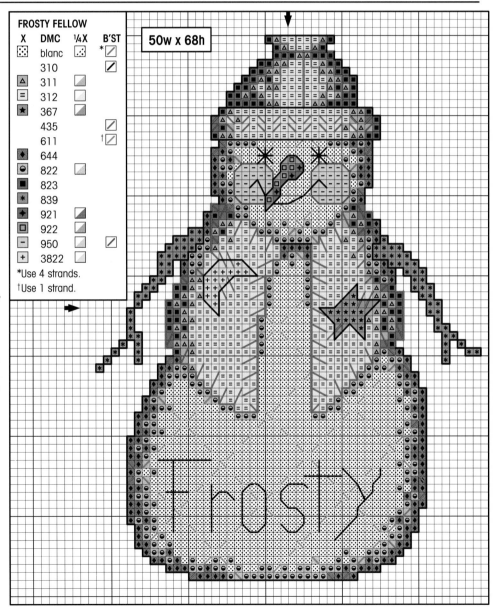

FROSTY FELLOW			
X	DMC	1/4X	B'ST
⊠	blanc	⊡	*◹
	310		◹
▲	311	◹	
=	312	◹	
★	367	◹	
	435		◹
	611		†◹
◆	644		
◑	822	◹	
■	823		
✳	839		
◆	921	◹	
▢	922	◹	
−	950	◹	◹
+	3822	◹	

*Use 4 strands.
†Use 1 strand.

50w x 68h

SUGARPLUM FANTASY DRESS (Shown on page 98)

You will need a girl's dress (we used a size 4T denim dress); white rickrack; 1/2 yd of 1 1/2"w satin ribbon; clear nylon thread; white, yellow, red, green, and brown acrylic paint; iridescent glitter, white, pink, red, purple, and light green dimensional fabric paint; acetate for stencils; stencil brushes or small sponge pieces; paintbrush; black permanent pen; 5/8"w red acrylic stars; small white buttons; craft knife and cutting mat; paper towels; removable tape (optional); jewel glue; and cardboard covered with waxed paper to fit inside bottom of dress.

1. Wash, dry, and press dress. Place cardboard in dress.
2. (**Note:** To stencil dress refer to **Stenciling** instructions, page 159.) Use patterns to make stencils. Overlapping ends of snowdrifts, stencil snowdrifts along bottom of dress. Stencil gingerbread boys, lollipops, candy canes, tree trunks, and trees on dress.
3. For gingerbread boys, use dimensional paint to paint pink cheeks and white wavy lines on arms and legs. Use pen to draw mouth and eyes. Glue on buttons.

4. For lollipops, use purple dimensional paint to paint spiral design. Use white dimensional paint to paint stick. Use paintbrush to paint over spiral design with glitter paint.
5. For candy canes, use red acrylic paint to paint stripes.
6. For trees, use light green dimensional paint to paint wavy lines on trees for branches. Glue 1 star to top of each tree.
7. For gumdrops and candy, use desired color of dimensional paint to paint gumdrops and candy. (Use additional coats of paint to make gumdrops desired thickness.) Paint over some gumdrops with glitter paint.
8. Paint over snowdrifts and around gingerbread boys with glitter paint.
9. For falling snow, use white dimensional paint to paint dots on dress.
10. Use nylon thread to sew rickrack along hem, cuffs, and collar of dress.
11. Tie ribbon into a bow; trim ends. Use a safety pin on inside of dress to pin bow at center of collar.

SANTA BOWL SHIRT

(Shown on page 96)

You will need a shirt large enough for an 11" dia. design, red fusible letters to spell "THE SANTA BOWL" and "NORTH POLE," acrylic paint (see Color Key), paintbrushes, tracing paper, transfer paper, red and black permanent pens, and a T-shirt form or cardboard covered with waxed paper.

1. Use Santa pattern and follow **Painting Techniques**, page 159, to paint Santa on shirt.
2. Arrange letters around Santa and fuse in place.

COLOR KEY
- white
- flesh
- dark flesh
- red
- dark red
- light green
- green
- dark green
- brown
- dark brown
- grey
- black

CANDY CANE

GINGERBREAD BOY

TREES

TREE TRUNK

LOLLIPOP

SNOWDRIFT

"DIAL 1-800 SANTA" CARDIGAN (Shown on page 97)

You will need a child's sweatshirt (we used a medium size), fabric for binding and button loop, thread to match fabric, a $5/8$" dia. shank button, acrylic paint (see Color Key), paintbrushes, black permanent pen, red and black fabric markers, removable fabric marking pen, tracing paper, transfer paper, and a T-shirt form or cardboard covered with waxed paper.

1. Wash, dry, and press cardigan and fabric.
2. For front opening of cardigan, use fabric marking pen and a yardstick to draw a line at center front of shirt from neck to bottom edge. Cut shirt open along marked line.
3. Cut off bottom ribbing and cuffs. For sleeve hem, press bottom edge of each sleeve $1/2$" to wrong side and stitch in place. Roll sleeves up to desired length.
4. For binding, measure bottom edge of cardigan. Cut a $2^1/2$"w bias fabric strip the determined measurement (piecing as necessary). Measure 1 front opening edge; add 1". Cut two $2^1/2$"w bias fabric strips the determined measurement.
5. Press ends of each front opening bias strip $1/2$" to wrong side. Press all 3 strips in half lengthwise with wrong sides together.
6. Matching raw edges, pin bottom binding along bottom edge on right side of cardigan. Using a $1/4$" seam allowance, sew binding to cardigan. Press binding over raw edges to wrong side of cardigan; pin in place. On right side of cardigan, stitch close to inner edge of binding, catching binding on wrong side of cardigan in stitching. Repeat to bind front opening edges of cardigan.
7. For button loop, press ends of a $1^1/2$" x 4" bias fabric strip $1/2$" to wrong side. Matching wrong sides, press strip in half lengthwise; unfold. Press long raw edges to center; refold. Stitch close to folded edges of strip. Form a loop from strip and sew ends to wrong side of cardigan at top of right opening edge (**Fig. 1**). Sew button to left front opening edge across from loop.

Fig. 1

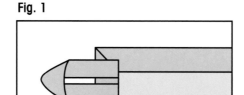

8. Use Santa pattern and follow **Painting Techniques**, page 159, to paint Santa on cardigan.
9. Trace words onto tracing paper. Use transfer paper to transfer words to cardigan. Use red marker to draw over words and black marker to draw phone cord.

JOLLY SANTA SWEATSHIRT
(Shown on page 98)

You will need an infant's sweatshirt (we used a 12-month size), one 6" square each of 10-mesh waste canvas and lightweight non-fusible interfacing, embroidery floss (see Color Key), masking tape, sewing thread, embroidery hoop (optional), tweezers, and a spray bottle filled with water.

Wash, dry, and press shirt. Follow Working on Waste Canvas, page 158, to stitch design on shirt. Use 4 strands of floss for Cross Stitch, 2 for Backstitch, and 3 for French Knots.

SANTA'S GARDEN WREATH SWEATSHIRT (Shown on page 97)

You will need a sweatshirt large enough for a 13" square design, acrylic paint (see Color Key), paintbrushes, black permanent pen, tracing paper, transfer paper, either a T-shirt form or cardboard covered with waxed paper to fit in shirt, and cardboard covered with waxed paper to fit in sleeve.

1. Use patterns and follow **Painting Techniques**, page 159, to paint Santa, bees, and words on shirt.
2. Use pen to draw dashed lines for bee trails.

JOLLY SANTA (26w x 26h)

X	DMC	B'ST	ANC.	COLOR
⊡	blanc	◢	2	white
◇	ecru		387	ecru
◼	310	◢	403	black
☆	320		215	lt green
◆	347		1025	red
✳	353		6	dk flesh
▲	367		217	green
+	415		398	grey
✕	676		891	lt gold
=	729		890	gold
◨	815		43	dk red
	898	◢	360	dk brown
⊡	948		1011	lt flesh
⊡	310		403	black Fr. knot

COLOR KEY

☐ white
▢ yellow
▢ flesh
▢ orange
▢ red
◼ dark red
▢ blue
▢ light green
▢ green
◼ dark green
▢ brown
▨ dark brown
▢ grey
▢ dark grey
◼ black

THE TASTES OF CHRISTMAS

Christmas is a time of merry music, colorful decorations, and — of course — — scrumptious foods. Whether you're planning a gala party, a simple down-home supper, or a flavorful coffeehouse sampling, we have the menus and recipes to make each gathering your most memorable ever! You'll discover so many delicious selections to indulge family members and share with neighbors that you'll turn to these recipes again and again! There's even a collection of gift-giving ideas featuring embellished stockings filled with homemade treats. Come savor the many tastes of Christmas!

OLD-TIME COUNTRY SUPPER

Come on in and sit right down to an old-time country supper! As the conversation unfolds over a spirited beverage and appetizer, it's soon time for the first course — creamy peanut soup and herb crackers. Next, the cranberry-glazed ham is carved, and homemade bread, warm from the oven, is brought to the table. Hearty helpings of succotash, green bean casserole, and baked sweet potatoes make this down-home meal more like a feast! To complete the evening, guests may sample old-fashioned treats with a cup of hot tea. It's easy to share your holiday hospitality with our Southern-style spread!

Basted with a sweet, tangy sauce, Fresh Ham with Cranberry Glaze is succulent and tender. It's sure to become traditional holiday fare.

FRESH HAM WITH CRANBERRY GLAZE

You may need to special order your ham (also called a pork leg) from the butcher.

1 fresh whole ham (about 14 pounds), trimmed
1½ cups chopped onions
¼ cup butter or margarine
2 cans (16 ounces each) whole berry cranberry sauce
⅔ cup apple cider vinegar
4 teaspoons Worcestershire sauce
¼ teaspoon hot pepper sauce
¾ cup firmly packed brown sugar
2 tablespoons dry mustard
1 tablespoon minced crystallized ginger

Preheat oven to 350 degrees. Place ham on a rack in a large roasting pan. Insert a meat thermometer into thickest portion of ham, making sure thermometer does not touch fat or bone. Cover and bake meat 18 to 20 minutes per pound or until thermometer registers 160 degrees.

For cranberry glaze, combine onions and butter in a medium saucepan; cook over medium heat about 10 minutes or until onions are tender. Stir in cranberry sauce, vinegar, Worcestershire sauce, and pepper sauce. Add brown sugar, dry mustard, and ginger; stir until well blended. Bring mixture to a boil. Reduce heat to medium-low; simmer 20 minutes or until mixture is slightly thickened. Uncover ham last hour of baking; spoon glaze over ham every 15 minutes. Remove from oven and allow to stand 15 minutes before serving. Serve warm with remaining cranberry glaze.
Yield: 28 to 35 servings

PEACH BRANDY CORDIAL

4½ cups water
4 cups peach nectar
1 can (12 ounces) frozen orange juice concentrate, thawed
1 can (12 ounces) frozen white grape juice concentrate, thawed
1 cup peach brandy
½ teaspoon anise extract

In a 1-gallon container, combine water, peach nectar, juice concentrates, brandy, and anise extract. Cover and chill. Serve chilled.
Yield: about 12½ cups cordial

A smooth before-dinner liqueur, Peach Brandy Cordial offers rich, fruity flavor with a hint of anise. Baked Onion Turnovers are tasty little treats featuring a sautéed onion filling in a golden brown pastry.

BAKED ONION TURNOVERS

PASTRY
2½ cups all-purpose flour
1 teaspoon dry mustard
½ teaspoon salt
⅛ teaspoon ground red pepper
2 packages (8 ounces each) cream cheese, softened
¾ cup butter or margarine, softened

FILLING
2 tablespoons butter or margarine
6 cups coarsely chopped yellow onions
2 tablespoons firmly packed brown sugar
½ teaspoon salt
¼ teaspoon ground black pepper
¼ teaspoon curry powder
⅛ teaspoon ground red pepper

For pastry, combine flour, dry mustard, salt, and red pepper in a medium bowl. Process cream cheese and butter in a food processor. Add dry ingredients to creamed mixture and process just until blended. Divide dough into fourths and wrap in plastic wrap; chill 1 hour.

Preheat oven to 375 degrees. For filling, melt butter in a large skillet over medium-high heat. Add onions; cook just until onions soften. Stir in brown sugar. Continue to cook until onions are lightly browned and sugar is dissolved; remove from heat. Stir in salt, black pepper, curry powder, and red pepper. Roll out one fourth of dough into a 9-inch square. Cut into 3-inch squares. Place about 1 rounded teaspoon onion mixture in center of each square. Fold dough over filling to form a triangle; use a fork to crimp edges together. Turn pastries over and crimp edges again. Prick tops of pastries with a fork. Transfer to a lightly greased baking sheet. Bake 15 to 20 minutes or until lightly browned. Repeat with remaining dough and filling. Serve warm.
Yield: about 3 dozen appetizers

115

Peanut butter, soy sauce, and chicken broth give Creamy Peanut Soup its unusual and robust taste. Buttery Parsley Crackers are a terrific accompaniment — and simple to make, too.

CREAMY PEANUT SOUP

1/4 cup butter or margarine
3/4 cup finely chopped onion
3/4 cup finely chopped celery
3 cloves garlic, minced
1/4 teaspoon crushed red pepper flakes
3 tablespoons all-purpose flour
6 cups chicken broth
1 1/2 cups smooth peanut butter
1 tablespoon soy sauce
Coarsely chopped peanuts to garnish

In a large saucepan, melt butter over medium-high heat. Add onion, celery, garlic, and red pepper flakes. Cook 5 minutes or until vegetables are tender. Sprinkle flour over vegetable mixture. Stirring constantly, cook 1 minute or until well blended. Whisking constantly, add chicken broth, peanut butter, and soy sauce. Reduce heat to medium-low; whisking frequently, simmer about 15 minutes. Garnish with peanuts and serve hot.
Yield: about 8 cups soup

PARSLEY CRACKERS

4 dozen saltine crackers
1/4 cup butter
3 tablespoons finely chopped fresh parsley

Preheat oven to 325 degrees. Place crackers on two 10 1/2 x 15 1/2-inch jellyroll pans. In a small saucepan, melt butter over medium heat. Remove from heat; stir in parsley. Brush butter mixture over crackers. Bake about 5 minutes or until lightly browned.
Yield: 4 dozen crackers

CORNMEAL-MOLASSES BREAD

Vegetable cooking spray
1 cup plus 6 teaspoons yellow cornmeal, divided
2 1/2 cups water
1/4 cup butter or margarine
2 teaspoons salt
1 package dry yeast
1/2 cup warm water
1/2 cup molasses
1 egg
5 to 6 cups all-purpose flour, divided

Spray two 1 1/2-quart ovenproof bowls with cooking spray. Sprinkle 2 teaspoons cornmeal in each bowl, turning to coat each bowl with cornmeal. In a medium saucepan, bring 2 1/2 cups water to a boil. Remove from heat; gradually whisk in 1 cup cornmeal. Add butter and salt; stir until butter melts. Let cornmeal mixture cool 30 minutes.

In a small bowl, dissolve yeast in 1/2 cup warm water. In a large bowl, combine cornmeal mixture, molasses, egg, and yeast mixture. Add 5 cups flour; stir until a soft dough forms. Turn dough onto a lightly floured surface. Knead about 5 minutes or until dough becomes smooth and elastic, using additional flour as necessary. Divide dough in half and place in prepared bowls. Spray tops of dough with cooking spray. Sprinkle remaining 2 teaspoons cornmeal on tops of loaves. Let bread rise uncovered in a warm place (80 to 85 degrees) 1 hour or until doubled in size.

Preheat oven to 375 degrees. Bake bread in bowls 43 to 50 minutes or until bread is golden brown and sounds hollow when tapped. Remove from bowls; serve warm or transfer to a wire rack to cool completely.
Yield: 2 round loaves

FESTIVE CABBAGE SLAW

11 cups finely shredded green cabbage
8 cups finely shredded Savoy cabbage
4 cups finely shredded Napa cabbage
2 1/4 cups finely chopped onions
1 cup finely chopped green pepper
1 cup finely chopped sweet red pepper
3/4 cup finely shredded carrots
2 cups sugar
1 1/4 cups apple cider vinegar
1/3 cup vegetable oil

Cornmeal-Molasses Bread *(clockwise from top left)* is a traditional yeast bread with a hearty texture. Cabbage, onion, peppers, and carrots are marinated in a tangy celery seed vinaigrette for Festive Cabbage Slaw. A twist on Waldorf salad, Apple-Pecan Salad features juicy apple bits, celery, raisins, and toasted pecans in a creamy mayonnaise dressing.

1 tablespoon salt
1 tablespoon celery seed
1 teaspoon dry mustard
¹/₂ teaspoon ground black pepper

In a very large bowl, combine cabbages, onions, peppers, and carrots. In a medium saucepan, combine sugar, vinegar, oil, salt, celery seed, dry mustard, and black pepper. Stirring frequently, cook over medium-high heat about 6 minutes or until mixture comes to a boil. Pour hot vinegar mixture over cabbage mixture. Toss until vegetables are well coated. Cover and chill 8 hours.
Yield: about 13 cups slaw

APPLE-PECAN SALAD

6 cups unpeeled, coarsely chopped
   apples
2 tablespoons lemon juice
¹/₂ cup finely chopped celery
¹/₂ cup raisins
¹/₂ cup chopped pecans, toasted
¹/₂ cup sour cream
¹/₂ cup mayonnaise
6 tablespoons sugar
   Red leaf lettuce to serve

In a large bowl, toss apples and lemon juice. Stir in celery, raisins, and pecans. In a small bowl, combine sour cream,

mayonnaise, and sugar. Stir sour cream mixture into apple mixture. Cover and chill until ready to serve.

To serve, spoon into a serving bowl lined with lettuce.
Yield: about 7 cups salad

117

CHRISTMAS SUCCOTASH

15 slices bacon
³/₄ cup finely chopped onion
2 packages (10 ounces each) frozen whole kernel yellow corn, thawed
2 packages (10 ounces each) frozen baby lima beans, thawed
1 can (10 ounces) diced tomatoes and green chiles
1¼ cups bread crumbs
2 cups half and half
3 eggs
1 tablespoon sugar
³/₄ teaspoon salt
¼ teaspoon ground black pepper

Preheat oven to 375 degrees. In a heavy large skillet, cook bacon over medium heat until crisp. Transfer bacon to paper towels, reserving drippings in skillet. Set aside 6 slices bacon for garnish; crumble remaining bacon. Cook onion in bacon drippings until tender; drain onion. In a large bowl, combine crumbled bacon, onion, corn, lima beans, undrained tomatoes and green chiles, and bread crumbs. In a small bowl, beat half and half and eggs until blended; stir in sugar, salt, and pepper. Stir half and half mixture into vegetable mixture. Pour into a greased 9 x 13-inch baking dish. Cover and bake 1½ hours. Uncover and bake 15 minutes longer. Crumble remaining bacon over casserole to garnish; serve warm.
Yield: 12 to 14 servings

GREEN BEAN AND MUSHROOM BAKE

1 can (10³/₄ ounces) golden mushroom soup
2 cups (8 ounces) shredded Swiss cheese, divided
1 cup sour cream
2 tablespoons white wine
½ teaspoon salt
½ teaspoon lemon pepper
¼ teaspoon ground black pepper
8 ounces fresh mushrooms, sliced
³/₄ cup finely chopped onion
1 clove garlic, minced
3 tablespoons butter or margarine
3 cans (14½ ounces each) French-style green beans, drained
¹/₃ cup coarsely chopped slivered almonds, toasted

Preheat oven to 325 degrees. In a medium bowl, combine soup, 1 cup cheese, sour cream, wine, salt, lemon

Twice-Baked Sweet Potatoes *(clockwise from top left on plate)* get their spicy flavor from a cinnamony topping and a filling of brown sugar, pineapple, and spices. Christmas Succotash is a colorful medley of favorite Southern vegetables sprinkled with crumbled bacon. Our delicious Green Bean and Mushroom Bake features sautéed mushrooms and a cheesy sour cream mixture. Slivered almonds lend a pleasing crunch to the casserole.

pepper, and black pepper. In a large skillet, sauté mushrooms, onion, and garlic in butter over medium heat just until vegetables are tender. Remove from heat and stir in green beans. Stir in soup mixture. Spoon mixture into a greased 9 x 13-inch baking dish. Sprinkle remaining 1 cup cheese over casserole. Sprinkle almonds over casserole. Bake 35 to 45 minutes or until casserole is heated through; serve warm.
Yield: 12 to 14 servings

TWICE-BAKED SWEET POTATOES

- 4 sweet potatoes
- ½ cup firmly packed brown sugar
- ¼ cup butter or margarine, softened
- 1 can (8 ounces) crushed pineapple, drained
- ¼ teaspoon ground cardamom
- ⅛ teaspoon ground ginger
- ⅛ teaspoon salt
- 1 cup bread crumbs
- ½ teaspoon ground cinnamon
- 2 tablespoons butter, melted

Preheat oven to 425 degrees. Trim ends and lightly grease potatoes. Bake 45 to 50 minutes or just until tender. Cool potatoes 30 minutes.

Preheat oven to 375 degrees. Cut potatoes in half lengthwise. Scoop out potato pulp, leaving about a ¼-inch shell. In a medium bowl, combine potato pulp, brown sugar, butter, pineapple, cardamom, ginger, and salt; beat until well blended and fluffy. Spoon potato mixture into potato shells and place on an ungreased baking sheet. In a small bowl, combine bread crumbs and cinnamon. Add melted butter; stir until well blended. Spoon over potatoes. Bake stuffed potatoes 20 minutes or until heated through and topping is golden brown. Serve warm.

Yield: 8 servings

RAGG WOOL MITTEN COOKIES

COOKIES

- 2 cups all-purpose flour
- 1 cup chopped pecans, toasted
- ¼ teaspoon salt
- 1 cup butter or margarine, softened
- ½ cup firmly packed brown sugar

ICING

- 1½ cups sifted confectioners sugar
- 3 tablespoons butter, softened
- 1 tablespoon plus 1 teaspoon milk
- 1 teaspoon vanilla extract
  Ivory, brown, red, terra-cotta, kelly green, and juniper green paste food coloring

For cookies, process flour, pecans, and salt in a food processor until mixture becomes a fine powder. In a large bowl, cream butter and brown sugar until fluffy. Add dry ingredients to creamed mixture; stir until a soft dough forms. Divide dough in half and wrap in plastic wrap; chill 4 hours.

Our Ragg Wool Mitten Cookies have the old-fashioned flavor of pecan shortbread. The mitten-shaped cookies are decorated with piped-on icing.

Preheat oven to 300 degrees. Trace pattern onto a piece of clear acetate; cut out. On a lightly floured surface, use a floured rolling pin to roll out half of dough to ¼-inch thickness. Place pattern on dough and use a sharp knife to cut out cookies. Transfer to a greased baking sheet. Bake 17 to 20 minutes or until bottoms are lightly browned. Cool cookies on baking sheet 3 minutes; transfer to a wire rack to cool completely. Repeat with remaining dough.

For icing, combine confectioners sugar, butter, milk, and vanilla in a small bowl; beat until smooth. Place ¼ cup icing in a small bowl; tint beige using ivory and brown food coloring. Divide remaining icing between 2 small bowls; tint one bowl "country red" using red and terra-cotta food coloring and tint remaining icing "country green" using kelly green and juniper green food coloring. Spoon icings into pastry bags fitted with small round tips. Pipe cuffs, hearts, and "blanket stitch" onto cookies. Use very small round tips to pipe lines and dots onto hearts. Pipe a circle of icing and fill in circle for each "button." Pipe icing onto top of each button for "thread." Allow icing to harden. Store in an airtight container in a single layer.

Yield: about 1½ dozen cookies

HOT CRANBERRY-LEMON TEA

8 cups boiling water
4 regular-size tea bags
1 stick cinnamon
1¼ cups sugar
4 cups cranberry juice cocktail
¼ cup freshly squeezed lemon juice
Cinnamon sticks to serve

In a heavy large Dutch oven, pour boiling water over tea bags and cinnamon stick; steep 5 minutes. Remove tea bags and cinnamon stick. Add sugar; stir until dissolved. Stir in cranberry juice cocktail and lemon juice. Place over medium heat until mixture is heated through. Serve hot with cinnamon sticks.
Yield: about 12 cups tea

FRUITED RICE CREAM

1 jar (6 ounces) red maraschino cherries, drained
1 jar (6 ounces) green maraschino cherries, drained
2⅓ cups milk
1 cup uncooked extra long-grain rice
⅛ teaspoon salt
2 cups miniature marshmallows
1 package (8 ounces) cream cheese, cut into small pieces and softened
½ cup sweetened condensed milk
½ teaspoon almond extract
½ teaspoon vanilla extract
2 cups whipping cream, whipped
½ cup sliced almonds

Chop cherries and drain on paper towels. Pat cherries dry and set aside. In a heavy medium saucepan, combine milk, rice, and salt over medium-low heat. Stirring frequently to prevent mixture from scorching, cover and cook about 25 to 30 minutes or until rice is tender and most of milk is absorbed. Remove from heat. Without stirring, add marshmallows and cream cheese to rice mixture; cover and let stand 5 minutes. Add sweetened condensed milk and extracts; stir until marshmallows melt and mixture is well blended. Transfer to a large bowl and cool 20 minutes.
Stir cherries into rice mixture. Fold in whipped cream and almonds. Spoon into individual serving dishes. Cover and chill until ready to serve.
Yield: about 8 cups fruited rice

Hot Cranberry-Lemon Tea is a citrusy beverage that's perfect for warming guests on cold winter nights. Light, fluffy Fruited Rice Cream is a dreamy concoction with maraschino cherries and sliced almonds.

A creamy custard crowns each moist, gooey layer of our Blackberry Jam Cake. This treat is so scrumptious, guests will insist on the recipe!

BLACKBERRY JAM CAKE

CAKE
- 1 cup butter or margarine, softened
- 2 cups sugar
- 4 eggs, separated
- 2 cups blackberry jam
- 3 cups all-purpose flour
- 1 teaspoon baking soda
- 1 teaspoon baking powder
- 1 teaspoon ground allspice
- 1 teaspoon ground cinnamon
- 1/8 teaspoon salt
- 1 cup buttermilk

CUSTARD
- 2 cups sugar
- 5 tablespoons all-purpose flour
- 1/8 teaspoon salt
- 1 1/2 cups milk
- 2 eggs
- 2 tablespoons butter or margarine
- 1 teaspoon vanilla extract
  Frozen whole blackberries to garnish

Preheat oven to 350 degrees. For cake, grease three 9-inch round cake pans and line bottoms with waxed paper; grease waxed paper. In a large bowl, cream butter and sugar until fluffy. Add egg yolks and jam; beat until smooth. In a medium bowl, combine flour, baking soda, baking powder, allspice, cinnamon, and salt. Alternately beat dry ingredients and buttermilk into creamed mixture, beating until well blended. In a small bowl, beat egg whites until stiff peaks form; fold into batter. Pour batter into prepared pans. Bake 28 to 33 minutes or until a toothpick inserted in center of cake comes out clean. Cool in pans 10 minutes. Remove from pans and cool completely on a wire rack.

For custard, combine sugar, flour, and salt in a heavy medium saucepan. Whisk in milk, eggs, and butter. Whisking constantly over medium heat, bring mixture to a boil; boil 2 minutes. Remove from heat. Stir in vanilla. Transfer mixture to a heatproof medium bowl. Set bowl in a larger bowl containing ice. Whisking occasionally, let mixture cool 10 minutes. Spread about 1 cup custard between each layer, spreading to edges. Spread remaining custard on top. Store in an airtight container in refrigerator. To serve, garnish with blackberries.

Yield: about 16 servings

121

CHRISTMAS PARADE

Everyone loves the jubilation of a Christmas parade — the brisk December air, the merry marching bands, and the elaborately decorated floats! After an exhilarating time watching the procession, invite the whole gang over for a family-style open house. What a perfect way to continue the fun! Start with toasty warm appetizers and a spirited punch, and then serve up cheesy quiche, colorful corn salad, hearty beef soup, and homemade rolls. This scrumptious collection offers lots of delicious alternatives for youngsters, too. Neighbors and friends will delight in this lighthearted affair!

An icy cold refreshment, Strawberry Wine Punch is a sweet accompaniment for these appetizers. Rolled in bread crumbs and baked until golden brown, Savory Party Bites *(bottom)* are tasty morsels made with sausage and cream cheese. Red pepper flavors the melt-in-your-mouth Sesame-Parmesan Rounds.

SAVORY PARTY BITES

- 1 pound hot pork sausage
- 1 package (8 ounces) cream cheese, softened
- ½ cup finely chopped onion
- ⅓ cup chopped fresh parsley
- 3 tablespoons prepared mustard
- ¼ teaspoon garlic powder
- 1 can (10 ounces) chopped sauerkraut, drained
- 4½ cups all-purpose baking mix
- 1¼ cups bread crumbs
- 2½ teaspoons paprika

In a food processor, combine uncooked sausage, cream cheese, onion, parsley, mustard, and garlic powder; process just until blended. Add sauerkraut; pulse process until blended. Transfer mixture to a large bowl. Stir in baking mix. Cover and chill 1 hour.

Preheat oven to 350 degrees. In a small bowl, combine bread crumbs and paprika. Shape sausage mixture into 1-inch balls. Roll each ball in bread crumb mixture. Place on a lightly greased baking sheet. Bake 23 to 26 minutes or until golden brown; serve warm.

Yield: about 8 dozen appetizers

SESAME-PARMESAN ROUNDS

- 2 cups all-purpose flour
- ½ teaspoon ground red pepper
- ⅛ teaspoon salt
- 1 cup butter, softened
- 1 cup freshly grated Parmesan cheese
- 1 egg white
- 1 teaspoon water
- ¼ cup sesame seed, toasted

Preheat oven to 350 degrees. In a medium bowl, combine flour, red pepper, and salt; set aside. In a large bowl, combine butter and cheese; beat until well blended. Add dry ingredients to creamed mixture; stir until well blended. On a lightly floured surface, use a floured rolling pin to roll out dough to ⅛-inch thickness. Use a 1½-inch biscuit cutter to cut out dough. Transfer to a greased baking sheet. In a small bowl, beat egg white and water until blended. Brush dough with egg white mixture and sprinkle with sesame seed. Bake 12 to 14 minutes or until bottoms are lightly browned. Serve warm or transfer to a wire rack to cool completely. Store in an airtight container.

To reheat crackers, place in a 325-degree oven about 2 minutes.

Yield: about 8 dozen crackers

A frothy beverage bursting with berry flavor, Strawberry Fizz offers a nonalcoholic alternative to our wine punch. The crowd-pleasing Layered Pizza Dip is a cheesy concoction topped with zesty pepperoni bits.

STRAWBERRY WINE PUNCH

- ½ cup sugar
- ¼ cup water
- 2 packages (10 ounces each) frozen sweetened sliced strawberries, partially thawed
- 2 bottles (750 ml each) red wine, chilled
- 1 bottle (2 liters) lemon-lime soda, chilled

In a small saucepan, combine sugar and water over medium-high heat. Stirring frequently, bring to a boil. Remove from heat and cool. Cover and chill syrup until ready to serve.

To serve, place strawberries in a 1½-gallon container. Pour wine and lemon-lime soda over strawberries; carefully stir to break up strawberries. Sweeten punch to taste by adding 1 tablespoon syrup at a time; stir well after each addition.

Yield: about 16 cups punch

STRAWBERRY FIZZ

- 3 packages (10 ounces each) frozen sweetened sliced strawberries
- 3 cartons (8 ounces each) strawberry yogurt
- 2 tablespoons sugar

- 4 cans (12 ounces each) strawberry-flavored soft drink, chilled

Process frozen strawberries, yogurt, and sugar in a food processor until smooth. Spoon strawberry mixture into a punch bowl; stir in soft drink.

Yield: about 16 cups punch

LAYERED PIZZA DIP

- 1 package (8 ounces) cream cheese, softened
- ½ cup sour cream
- ¼ cup freshly grated Parmesan cheese
- ½ teaspoon garlic salt
- ½ cup prepared pizza sauce
- ¾ cup shredded mozzarella cheese
- 1 package (3.5 ounces) sliced pepperoni, finely chopped
  Toasted pita bread wedges to serve

Preheat oven to 350 degrees. In a small bowl, beat cream cheese until fluffy. Stir in sour cream, Parmesan cheese, and garlic salt. Spread into a lightly greased 9-inch pie plate. Spread pizza sauce over cream cheese mixture. Sprinkle mozzarella cheese over pizza sauce and top with pepperoni. Bake about 20 minutes or until heated through. Serve warm with pita bread.

Yield: about 3 cups dip

CORN SALAD WITH ROASTED GARLIC DRESSING

1 head garlic (about 10 to 14 cloves)
  Olive oil
²/₃ cup mayonnaise
¹/₂ cup chopped fresh parsley
1 tablespoon Greek seasoning
4 cans (15¹/₄ ounces each) whole kernel yellow corn, drained
2 cups chopped sweet red pepper
1¹/₂ cups chopped green onions

Preheat oven to 400 degrees. To roast garlic, slightly trim tops of garlic cloves. Place garlic head on aluminum foil. Drizzle a small amount of oil on cut edges; wrap in foil. Bake 1 hour. Cool completely.

Press garlic pulp out of each clove and mash in a small bowl. Add mayonnaise, parsley, and Greek seasoning; stir until well blended. In a large bowl, combine corn, red pepper, and green onions; toss with garlic dressing. Cover and chill 2 hours before serving.
Yield: about 9 cups salad

FOUR-CHEESE QUICHES

1 container (15 ounces) ricotta cheese
11 ounces cream cheese, softened
9 eggs
3 tablespoons chopped fresh parsley
1 tablespoon stone-ground mustard
¹/₃ cup freshly grated Parmesan cheese
2 tablespoons all-purpose flour
1 teaspoon baking powder
¹/₂ teaspoon salt
3 cups (12 ounces) shredded Jarlsberg cheese

Preheat oven to 350 degrees. In a large bowl, beat ricotta cheese and cream cheese until blended. Beat in eggs, parsley, and mustard. In a small bowl, combine Parmesan cheese, flour, baking powder, and salt. Stir dry ingredients into egg mixture; beat until well blended. Stir in Jarlsberg cheese. Pour into 2 greased 9-inch deep-dish pie plates. Bake 33 to 38 minutes or until a knife inserted near center of quiche comes out clean. Allow to stand 10 minutes before serving.
Yield: 2 quiches, about 8 servings each

Corn Salad with Roasted Garlic Dressing delights the senses with a confetti of corn, sweet red peppers, and green onions tossed in a zippy dressing. Four-Cheese Quiche is so cheesy and good, guests will eat it up!

OVEN-BAKED MINESTRONE SOUP

1½ pounds stew beef, cut into
      small pieces
1 cup chopped onion
2 cloves garlic, minced
2 tablespoons olive oil
1 teaspoon salt
1 teaspoon ground black pepper
3 cans (14.5 ounces each) beef broth
2¾ cups water
1 can (16 ounces) kidney beans
1 can (14.5 ounces) diced stewed
      tomatoes
1½ cups thinly sliced carrots
1 can (6 ounces) whole pitted ripe
      olives
2 cups sliced zucchini
1 cup uncooked small elbow
      macaroni
½ teaspoon dried basil leaves
¼ teaspoon dried thyme leaves
¼ teaspoon dried oregano leaves
¼ teaspoon dried rosemary leaves
¼ teaspoon ground savory
      Freshly shredded Parmesan cheese
      to serve

Preheat oven to 400 degrees. In a large ovenproof Dutch oven, combine beef, onion, garlic, oil, salt, and pepper. Stirring occasionally, bake uncovered 45 minutes. Leaving soup in oven, reduce heat to 350 degrees. Combine beef broth and water in a 2-quart microwave-safe container. Microwave on high power (100%) 10 minutes or until broth mixture begins to boil; add to beef mixture. Stir in undrained beans, undrained tomatoes, carrots, and undrained olives. Cover and bake about 2 hours or until meat is tender. Stir in zucchini, macaroni, and herbs; cover and bake 30 minutes longer or until vegetables are tender. To serve, sprinkle each serving with cheese.
Yield: about 15 cups soup

OLD-FASHIONED YEAST ROLLS

1 cup warm milk
1 cup warm water
2 packages dry yeast
1 tablespoon sugar
4 to 5 cups all-purpose flour,
      divided
3 tablespoons butter or margarine,
      melted
2 teaspoons salt
      Vegetable cooking spray
1 egg, beaten
1 tablespoon milk

Serve Oven-Baked Minestrone Soup for the perfect winter warmer! Its beefy stock base is loaded with vegetables, beans, pasta, and whole black olives. Light and fluffy, Old-fashioned Yeast Rolls are just like the ones Grandma would have made. Or for a flavorful change from dinner rolls, try our easy-to-make Crunchy Breadstick Streamers.

In a large bowl, combine warm milk and water, yeast, sugar, and 1 cup flour. Beat mixture until well blended and smooth. Cover and let rise in a warm place (80 to 85 degrees) 1 hour or until doubled in size.

Stir melted butter and salt into yeast mixture. Add 3 cups flour; stir until a soft dough forms. Turn dough onto a lightly floured surface. Knead about 5 minutes or until dough becomes smooth and elastic, using additional flour as necessary. Place in a large bowl sprayed with cooking spray, turning once to coat top of dough. Cover and let rise in a warm place about 2 hours or until tripled in size.

Turn dough onto a lightly floured surface and punch down. Shape dough into 2-inch rolls. Place 2 inches apart on a greased baking sheet. Spray tops of rolls with cooking spray. Cover and let rise in a warm place 1 hour or until almost doubled in size.

Preheat oven to 375 degrees. In a small bowl, combine egg and milk. Brush rolls with egg mixture. Bake 20 to 25 minutes or until rolls are lightly browned. Serve warm or transfer to a wire rack to cool completely.
Yield: about 2 dozen rolls

CRUNCHY BREADSTICK STREAMERS

2 cans (2.8 ounces each) French-
      fried onions, crushed
1 egg, lightly beaten
2 tablespoons milk
1 can (11 ounces) refrigerated
      breadstick dough

Preheat oven to 350 degrees. Place crushed onions on a piece of aluminum foil. In a small bowl, combine egg and milk. Without separating strips, unroll dough onto a flat surface. Cut dough in half crosswise. Brush both sides of dough pieces with egg mixture. Separate dough at perforations to form 16 strips. Roll each strip in onions, lightly pressing onions into dough. Place on a greased baking sheet; twist ends in opposite directions. Bake 13 to 15 minutes or until golden brown. Serve warm.
Yield: 16 breadsticks

RASPBERRY-CHOCOLATE CAKE

CAKE
- 1 cup cocoa
- 2 cups boiling water
- 1 cup butter or margarine, softened
- 2½ cups sugar
- 4 eggs
- 1½ teaspoons vanilla extract
- 2¾ cups sifted all-purpose flour
- 2 teaspoons baking soda
- ½ teaspoon baking powder
- ½ teaspoon salt

FILLING
- 3½ cups sifted confectioners sugar
- 6 tablespoons butter or margarine, softened
- 6 tablespoons raspberry-flavored liqueur

ICING
- 1 package (6 ounces) semisweet chocolate chips
- 1 cup butter or margarine
- ½ cup half and half
- 2½ cups sifted confectioners sugar
  Gumdrop raspberry candies and silk leaves to garnish

Preheat oven to 350 degrees. For cake, grease and lightly flour three 9-inch round cake pans. In a medium bowl, combine cocoa and boiling water; whisk until smooth. Cool cocoa mixture completely.

In a large bowl, cream butter and sugar until fluffy. Add eggs and vanilla; beat until smooth. In a medium bowl, combine flour, baking soda, baking powder, and salt. Alternately beat dry ingredients and cocoa mixture into creamed mixture just until blended (do not overbeat). Pour batter into prepared pans. Bake 25 to 30 minutes or until a toothpick inserted in center of cake comes out clean. Cool in pans 10 minutes. Remove from pans and cool completely on a wire rack.

For filling, beat confectioners sugar, butter, and liqueur in a medium bowl until smooth and fluffy. Spread filling evenly between layers. Chill 2 hours.

For icing, combine chocolate chips, butter, and half and half in a medium saucepan over medium heat. Stirring constantly, cook about 6 to 8 minutes or until mixture is smooth. Remove from heat and whisk in confectioners sugar. Transfer icing to a medium bowl placed over a bowl of ice; beat about 8 minutes or until icing holds its shape. Spread icing on top and sides of cake, using back of a spoon to swirl icing. Place in

Rich Raspberry-Chocolate Cake features a creamy filling kissed with fruit-flavored liqueur. Topped with a buttery brown sugar and pecan mixture, luscious Praline Pumpkin Cheesecake is an updated version of the traditional holiday pumpkin pie.

an airtight container in refrigerator until ready to serve. To serve, garnish with candies and leaves.

Yield: about 16 servings

PRALINE PUMPKIN CHEESECAKE

CRUST
- ⅔ cup graham cracker crumbs
- ⅔ cup gingersnap cookie crumbs
- 2 tablespoons butter or margarine, melted

TOPPING
- 1 cup firmly packed brown sugar
- 6 tablespoons butter or margarine, softened
- 1 cup coarsely chopped pecans

FILLING
- 3 packages (8 ounces each) cream cheese, softened
- ½ cup granulated sugar
- ½ cup firmly packed brown sugar
- 1 can (15 ounces) pumpkin
- 4 eggs
- ¼ cup evaporated milk
- 3 tablespoons all-purpose flour
- 2 tablespoons maple syrup
- 2 teaspoons pumpkin pie spice

For crust, combine cracker and cookie crumbs and butter in a small bowl. Press mixture into bottom of a lightly greased 10-inch springform pan.

For topping, combine brown sugar and butter in a small bowl. Stir in pecans.

Preheat oven to 325 degrees. For filling, beat cream cheese and sugars in a large bowl until fluffy. Beat in remaining ingredients until smooth; pour over crust. With rack in center of oven, bake cake about 1½ hours or until sides pull away from pan and center is almost set. Sprinkle topping over cake; bake 10 minutes longer. Leaving cake on same rack, broil 1 to 2 minutes or until sugar caramelizes and edges of cheesecake are golden brown. Cool in pan to room temperature on a wire rack. Remove sides of pan and serve.
Yield: about 16 servings

CONFETTI SNACK MIX

- 1 package (22 ounces) jelly beans
- 1 package (14 ounces) star-shaped milk chocolate candies
- 1 package (10 ounces) mini peanut butter sandwich cookies
- 4 cups small pretzel twists
- 4 cups bite-size frosted wheat cereal

In a very large bowl, combine all ingredients. Store in an airtight container.
Yield: about 16 cups snack mix

Eaten by the handfuls, quick-and-easy Confetti Snack Mix combines store-bought candies, cookies, and cereal. A sweet treat for dunking apple slices, Minty Marshmallow Fruit Dip is a combination of three simple ingredients. Kids will love ooey, gooey S'More Chocolate Bars! Graham cracker crumbs, chocolate chips, and miniature marshmallows top this brownie-based goody.

S'MORE CHOCOLATE BARS

- 1 package (21.1 ounces) brownie mix
- ½ cup vegetable oil
- ½ cup water
- 1 egg
- 7 graham crackers (2½ x 5-inch rectangles), coarsely crumbled
- 1½ cups semisweet chocolate chips
- 3 cups miniature marshmallows

Preheat oven to 350 degrees. In a large bowl, combine brownie mix, oil, water, and egg; stir until well blended. Pour into a greased 9 x 13-inch baking pan. Sprinkle graham cracker crumbs over batter. Bake 20 minutes. Sprinkle chocolate chips over brownies; top with marshmallows. Bake 8 to 10 minutes longer or until marshmallows begin to brown. Cool in pan on a wire rack. Use an oiled knife to cut into 1 x 2-inch bars. Store in an airtight container.
Yield: about 4 dozen bars

MINTY MARSHMALLOW FRUIT DIP

- 1 package (8 ounces) cream cheese, softened
- 1 jar (7 ounces) marshmallow creme
- ¼ cup finely crushed peppermint candies
- Crushed peppermint candies to garnish
- Apple slices to serve

In a medium bowl, beat cream cheese until fluffy. Add marshmallow creme; beat mixture until well blended. Stir in finely crushed peppermint candies. Store in an airtight container in refrigerator.

To serve, garnish dip with crushed peppermint candies. Serve with apple slices.
Yield: about 1¾ cups fruit dip

DECK THE HALLS

Enticing family and friends to help with your holiday decorating will be fun and easy with our delicious party menu. The brunch-time fare includes tasty morsels to snack on while everyone decks the halls, as well as sit-down-to-eat dishes — and it's all low-fat! These scrumptious offerings are hearty enough to satisfy the biggest appetites, yet healthy enough that you'll all still fit into your elf suits!

For a refreshing zing, Champagne Punch combines fruit juices, brandy, and chilled bubbly. Cheesy Artichoke-Parmesan Puffs are great grab-as-you-go appetizers, and Light Cucumber-Dill Dip will be a crowd pleaser.

CHAMPAGNE PUNCH

1 bottle (64 ounces) cranberry juice cocktail, chilled
1 can (12 ounces) frozen pineapple juice concentrate, thawed
2 cups brandy
2 bottles (750 ml each) champagne, chilled

Combine all ingredients except champagne in a large punch bowl. Stir in champagne. Serve immediately.
Yield: about 18 cups punch

1 serving (6 ounces): 164 calories, 0.1 gram fat, 0.3 gram protein, 19.7 grams carbohydrate

ARTICHOKE-PARMESAN PUFFS

1 cup water
2 tablespoons reduced-calorie margarine
1 cup all-purpose flour
1 teaspoon garlic salt
1/2 cup egg substitute
1 egg
1 can (14 ounces) artichoke hearts, drained and finely chopped
1/4 cup grated fat-free Parmesan cheese

Preheat oven to 375 degrees. Bring water and margarine to a boil in a large saucepan. Reduce heat to low. Add flour and garlic salt all at once, stirring vigorously until mixture forms a ball; remove from heat. Add egg substitute and egg; beat until well blended. Beat in artichoke hearts and cheese. Drop heaping teaspoons of batter onto a baking sheet lined with parchment paper. Bake 25 to 28 minutes or until lightly browned. Serve warm.
Yield: about 5 dozen appetizers

1 serving (1 appetizer): 17 calories, 0.4 gram fat, 0.7 gram protein, 2.6 grams carbohydrate

LIGHT CUCUMBER-DILL DIP

4 ounces fat-free cream cheese
1/2 cup fat-free cottage cheese
1 tablespoon chopped green onion
2 teaspoons freshly squeezed lemon juice
3/4 teaspoon salt
1/2 teaspoon chopped fresh dill weed
1/8 teaspoon ground black pepper
1 cucumber peeled, seeded, and coarsely chopped
Fresh vegetables to serve

Replace traditional stuffing with zesty Caesar Bread Salad — a colorful concoction of fresh tomatoes, cucumber, and herbed stuffing.

Process cream cheese, cottage cheese, green onion, lemon juice, salt, dill weed, and black pepper in a food processor until smooth. Add cucumber; pulse process just until blended. Cover and chill 2 hours to allow flavors to blend. Serve with fresh vegetables.
Yield: about 2 cups dip

1 serving (1 tablespoon dip):
7 calories, 0 gram fat, 1.1 grams protein, 0.7 gram carbohydrate

CAESAR BREAD SALAD

1 package (8 ounces) herb-seasoned stuffing
5 cups chopped fresh tomatoes

1 1/2 cups shredded unpeeled cucumber
1 cup chopped fresh parsley
1 cup fat-free Caesar salad dressing
1 tablespoon balsamic vinegar
1 tablespoon olive oil

Combine stuffing, tomatoes, cucumber, and parsley; stir gently. In a small bowl, combine salad dressing, vinegar, and oil. Stir dressing mixture into salad. Cover and chill 2 hours; serve within 4 hours.
Yield: about 18 servings

1 serving (1/2 cup): 82 calories, 1.4 grams fat, 2.0 grams protein, 15.3 grams carbohydrate

Creamy Celery Soup, seasoned with tarragon, and homemade Parmesan Bread Sticks are two terrific starts to this festive affair.

CREAMY CELERY SOUP

- 6 cups coarsely chopped celery
- 5 cups peeled and coarsely chopped potatoes
- 1 cup chopped green onions
- 3 cans (14.5 ounces each) fat-free chicken broth
- 2 tablespoons freshly squeezed lemon juice
- 1 teaspoon dried tarragon leaves
- 3/4 teaspoon salt
- 1/2 teaspoon ground white pepper
- 1 cup plain low-fat yogurt
- 2 teaspoons cornstarch
  Celery leaves to garnish

In a large Dutch oven, combine celery, potatoes, onions, and chicken broth. Cover and cook over medium-low heat 1 hour or until vegetables are tender. Reserving broth, use a slotted spoon to transfer vegetables to a food processor; purée vegetables. Return puréed vegetables to broth in Dutch oven. Stir in lemon juice, tarragon leaves, salt, and white pepper. Cover and cook over medium-low heat 10 minutes or until mixture begins to simmer (do not boil).

Remove soup from heat. In a small bowl, whisk yogurt and cornstarch until well blended. Gradually stir yogurt mixture into soup. Garnish with celery leaves. Serve immediately.
Yield: about 12 cups soup

1 serving (3/4 cup): 69 calories, 0.7 gram fat, 2.9 grams protein, 13.6 grams carbohydrate

PARMESAN BREAD STICKS

- 1 package dry yeast
- 1 teaspoon sugar
- 1 1/4 cups warm water
- 2 1/2 to 2 3/4 cups all-purpose flour, divided
- 1/2 teaspoon salt
- 1 tablespoon olive oil
  Vegetable cooking spray
- 2 tablespoons freshly grated Parmesan cheese

In a small bowl, dissolve yeast and sugar in warm water. In a large bowl, combine 1 cup flour and salt. Add yeast mixture and oil to dry ingredients; beat with an electric mixer about 3 minutes. Add 1 1/2 cups flour; stir until well blended. Turn dough onto a lightly floured surface. Knead about 5 minutes or until dough becomes smooth and elastic, using remaining flour as necessary. Place in a large bowl sprayed with cooking spray, turning once to coat top of dough. Cover and let rise in a warm place (80 to 85 degrees) 1 hour or until doubled in size.

Turn dough onto a lightly floured surface and punch down. Roll dough into a 12 x 16-inch rectangle. Cut dough into 1 x 12-inch strips. Twist and press ends onto an ungreased baking sheet. Lightly brush strips with water. Sprinkle with Parmesan cheese. Lightly cover strips and let rise in a warm place 45 minutes or until almost doubled in size.

Preheat oven to 400 degrees. Bake 12 to 17 minutes or until bottoms are lightly browned. Serve warm.
Yield: 16 bread sticks

1 serving (1 bread stick): 92 calories, 1.3 grams fat, 2.7 grams protein, 16.9 grams carbohydrate

CRANBERRY-PEAR AMBROSIA

1¼ cups 2% milk, divided
2 tablespoons cornstarch
¼ cup sugar
½ cup frozen unsweetened shredded coconut, thawed
3 cups unpeeled, cored, and coarsely chopped red pears
⅔ cup sweetened dried cranberries
1 tablespoon frozen unsweetened flaked coconut, thawed and toasted to garnish

In a small bowl, combine ¼ cup milk and cornstarch; stir until smooth. In a medium saucepan, combine sugar and remaining 1 cup milk; bring to a simmer over medium heat. Whisking constantly, add cornstarch mixture; cook until sauce thickens. Remove from heat; cool.

Stir in ½ cup coconut. Gently combine coconut sauce, pears, and cranberries. Cover and refrigerate until well chilled. Garnish with toasted coconut.
Yield: about 8 servings

1 serving (½ cup): 135 calories, 3.9 grams fat, 1.8 grams protein, 24.5 grams carbohydrate

HAM HASH

Vegetable cooking spray
1 cup chopped onion
4 cups diced unpeeled red potatoes
2 cups thinly sliced and chopped low-fat ham
1 can (4.5 ounces) chopped green chiles
¼ cup low-fat sour cream
¾ teaspoon garlic salt
½ teaspoon ground cumin

Spray a large nonstick skillet with cooking spray. Sauté onion in skillet over medium-high heat until onion is tender and begins to brown. Reduce heat to medium. Stir in potatoes. Stirring occasionally, cook about 25 minutes or until potatoes are golden brown and almost tender. Stir in ham, undrained chiles, sour cream, garlic salt, and cumin. Stirring occasionally, cook about 5 minutes or until mixture is heated through. Serve warm.
Yield: about 11 servings

1 serving (½ cup): 91 calories, 2.0 grams fat, 6.4 grams protein, 11.9 grams carbohydrate

A fruit-lover's delight, Cranberry-Pear Ambrosia *(bottom)* is served in a dreamy coconut sauce. Bits of lean ham and diced potatoes make Ham Hash *(left)* a hearty yet healthy main dish. Chiles, onion, and cumin give the casserole its spicy flavor.

BRUSSELS SPROUTS WITH LIGHT ORANGE SAUCE

3 pounds fresh Brussels sprouts
3/4 cup freshly squeezed orange juice
6 tablespoons fat-free Italian salad
   dressing
1 1/2 teaspoons grated orange zest
   Grated orange zest to garnish

Trim Brussels sprouts and cut an "X" in stem end of each sprout. Place in a steamer basket over simmering water. Cover and steam about 15 minutes or until sprouts are tender. In a small bowl, combine orange juice, salad dressing, and 1 1/2 teaspoons orange zest. Toss sprouts with orange sauce. Transfer to a serving dish. Garnish with orange zest. Serve warm.
Yield: about 16 servings

1 serving (1/2 cup): 45 calories, 0.3 gram fat, 3.0 grams protein, 9.4 grams carbohydrate

BACON-CHEESE RISOTTO

2 cans (14.5 ounces each) fat-free
   chicken broth
3 cups water
   Vegetable cooking spray
1 package (8 ounces) fresh
   mushrooms, sliced
1 1/4 cups chopped sweet red pepper
2 teaspoons minced garlic
2 cups uncooked Arborio rice
1/2 teaspoon salt
1 cup (4 ounces) shredded reduced-
   fat sharp Cheddar cheese
6 slices turkey bacon, cooked and
   crumbled

Combine broth and water in a medium saucepan; bring to a simmer (do not boil). Keep warm. In a large saucepan sprayed with cooking spray, sauté mushrooms, red pepper, and garlic over medium-high heat about 5 minutes or until tender. Stirring constantly, add rice and cook 2 minutes. Reduce heat to medium-low. Add salt and 1 cup broth mixture; stir constantly until most of liquid is absorbed. Add remaining broth mixture, 1/2 cup at a time, stirring after each addition until liquid is absorbed and rice has a creamy consistency (about 35 minutes). Stir in cheese and bacon; serve immediately.
Yield: about 15 servings

1 serving (1/2 cup): 119 calories, 1.8 grams fat, 5.7 grams protein, 20.1 grams carbohydrate

Brussels Sprouts with Light Orange Sauce are splashed with subtle citrus goodness. A traditional Italian specialty consisting of rice, vegetables, and broth, our Bacon-Cheese Risotto uses reduced-fat Cheddar cheese and turkey bacon for a tasty low-fat combination. Tart and tangy Congealed Beets and Carrots will make an eye-catching addition to the table.

CONGEALED BEETS AND CARROTS

1 jar (16 ounces) pickled beets
1 package (3 ounces) lemon gelatin
1 cup hot water
1 tablespoon apple cider vinegar
1/4 teaspoon salt
2/3 cup diced celery
2/3 cup finely shredded carrots
1 tablespoon grated onion
2 teaspoons prepared horseradish
1/8 teaspoon ground black pepper
   Carrot curl to garnish

Reserving liquid, drain beets and chop. Add water to reserved beet liquid to make 1 cup. Place gelatin in a medium bowl. Add hot water; stir until dissolved. Add beet liquid, vinegar, and salt. Chill about 45 minutes or until slightly thickened.

Fold in beets, celery, carrots, onion, horseradish, and pepper. Pour into an oiled 1-quart mold. Cover and chill until firm.

To serve, dip mold into warm water 10 seconds; invert onto a serving plate. Garnish with carrot curl.
Yield: about 8 servings

1 serving (1/2 cup): 84 calories, 0.1 gram fat, 1.5 grams protein, 20.5 grams carbohydrate

Delectable Salmon-Cream Cheese Crêpes have a rich seafood filling. The elegant creations can be prepared ahead of time and baked just before serving.

SALMON-CREAM CHEESE CRÊPES

Crêpes can be assembled ahead of time and refrigerated.

CRÊPES
- ²/₃ cup all-purpose flour
- ¹/₄ teaspoon salt
- ¹/₄ teaspoon ground white pepper
- 1 cup evaporated skimmed milk
- 1 egg
- 1 tablespoon reduced-calorie margarine, melted
- Vegetable cooking spray

FILLING
- 1 package (8 ounces) fat-free cream cheese, softened
- 2 tablespoons finely chopped green onions
- 1¹/₂ tablespoons drained capers, rinsed
- 1 teaspoon dried basil leaves
- ¹/₄ teaspoon garlic powder
- ¹/₄ teaspoon ground white pepper
- 3 packages (3 ounces each) smoked salmon, broken into pieces
- Chopped green onion to garnish

For crêpes, combine flour, salt, and white pepper in a medium bowl. Add evaporated milk, egg, and melted margarine; whisk until smooth. Cover and chill 30 minutes.

Lightly spray an 8-inch nonstick skillet with cooking spray. Place pan over medium heat until hot. For each crêpe, spoon about 2 tablespoons batter into pan. Tilt pan to spread batter evenly over bottom of pan to form a 5-inch circle.

Cook until lightly browned; turn over and cook 30 seconds longer. Place crêpes between layers of waxed paper.

For filling, combine cream cheese, 2 tablespoons chopped green onions, capers, basil, garlic powder, and white pepper in a medium bowl. Gently stir in salmon. Fill each crêpe with about 2 tablespoons salmon mixture. Roll up crêpes and place, seam side down, in a 9 x 13-inch baking dish. Cover and store crêpes in refrigerator until ready to serve.

To serve, bake covered 20 minutes in a 350-degree oven. Garnish with green onion and serve warm.

Yield: about 12 crêpes

1 serving (1 crêpe): 97 calories, 2.1 grams fat, 9.7 grams protein, 9.2 grams carbohydrate

For a light and luscious dessert, try Baked Honey Fruit. Served with a dollop of whipped topping, Spiced Irish Coffee is a spirited holiday beverage — and a great accompaniment to Blueberry Tea Buns. These wholesome scone-like treats are bursting with fruit.

BAKED HONEY FRUIT

- 1 can (20 ounces) pineapple chunks in juice
- 2 tablespoons cornstarch
- 1 jar (6 ounces) maraschino cherries, drained
- 1 1/2 cups coarsely chopped orange sections
- 1 1/2 cups coarsely chopped grapefruit sections
- 1/3 cup honey
- 4 fresh mint leaves, chopped
  Fresh mint leaves to garnish

Preheat oven to 375 degrees. Reserving juice, drain pineapple. In a small bowl, dissolve cornstarch in reserved pineapple juice. In a medium bowl, combine pineapple, cherries, orange, grapefruit, honey, and chopped mint leaves. Stir in cornstarch mixture. Pour fruit mixture into a 9-inch square baking dish. Bake 1 hour or until mixture is thick and bubbly. Garnish each serving with mint leaves. Serve warm.
Yield: about 9 servings

1 serving (1/2 cup): 128 calories, 0.2 gram fat, 0.8 gram protein, 33.9 grams carbohydrate

BLUEBERRY TEA BUNS

- 1/3 cup plus 1 tablespoon sugar, divided
- 1 3/4 cups all-purpose flour
- 1 teaspoon ground cinnamon
- 1 teaspoon baking soda
- 1/2 teaspoon salt
- 1 can (8 ounces) crushed pineapple in juice, lightly drained
- 1/4 cup skim milk
- 3 tablespoons vegetable oil
- 1/4 cup egg substitute
- 1 1/2 cups frozen blueberries (do not thaw)
  Vegetable cooking spray

Preheat oven to 400 degrees. In a medium bowl, combine 1/3 cup sugar, flour, cinnamon, baking soda, and salt; make a well in center of mixture. Combine pineapple, milk, oil, and egg substitute; add to dry ingredients. Stir just until dry ingredients are moistened. Gently stir in blueberries. Drop batter by heaping tablespoonfuls onto a baking sheet sprayed with cooking spray. Sprinkle remaining 1 tablespoon sugar over batter. Bake 12 to 15 minutes or until golden brown. Serve warm.
Yield: about 24 muffins

1 serving (1 muffin): 75 calories, 2.0 grams fat, 1.4 grams protein, 13.1 grams carbohydrate

SPICED IRISH COFFEE

- 1/3 cup plus 2 tablespoons sugar, divided
- 1/4 teaspoon ground cinnamon
- 2 cups skim milk
- 2 cinnamon sticks
- 1 whole nutmeg, crushed
- 2 1/2 quarts hot, strongly brewed coffee
- 3 tablespoons fat-free non-dairy powdered creamer
- 2/3 cup Irish whiskey
  Fat-free frozen whipped topping, thawed to garnish

Combine 2 tablespoons sugar and ground cinnamon; set aside. Combine remaining 1/3 cup sugar, milk, cinnamon sticks, and nutmeg in a Dutch oven. Cook over medium-low heat, stirring until sugar dissolves. Stir in coffee and creamer. Cover and heat 5 minutes to allow flavors to blend. Remove from heat; strain and discard cinnamon sticks and nutmeg. Stir in Irish whiskey. Pour into 8-ounce Irish coffee glasses. Garnish each serving with 1 tablespoon whipped topping and sprinkle with sugar-cinnamon mixture. Serve immediately.
Yield: about 12 cups coffee

1 serving (8 ounces): 91 calories, 0.1 gram fat, 1.6 grams protein, 13.5 grams carbohydrate

CHOCOLATE-CINNAMON ROLLS

DOUGH

- 1 package quick-acting dry yeast
- 1 cup warm water
- 2¾ cups all-purpose flour
- ½ cup cocoa
- ½ cup sugar
- 1 teaspoon salt
- ¼ cup egg substitute
- 1½ tablespoons vegetable oil
  Vegetable cooking spray

FILLING

- 3 tablespoons sugar, divided
- 4 teaspoons ground cinnamon, divided
- 3 tablespoons reduced-calorie margarine, divided
- 1⅓ cups reduced-fat chocolate chips, divided
  Vegetable cooking spray

GLAZE

- ½ cup sifted confectioners sugar
- 2 teaspoons water

For dough, dissolve yeast in 1 cup warm water in a small bowl. In a large bowl, combine flour, cocoa, sugar, and salt. Add egg substitute, oil, and yeast mixture to dry ingredients; stir until a soft dough forms. Turn onto a lightly floured surface and knead about 3 minutes or until dough becomes smooth and elastic. Place in a large bowl sprayed with cooking spray, turning once to coat top of dough. Cover and let rise in a warm place (80 to 85 degrees) 1 hour or until almost doubled in size.

For filling, combine 1½ tablespoons sugar and 2 teaspoons cinnamon in a small bowl; set aside. Turn dough onto a lightly floured surface and punch down. Divide dough in half. Roll out half of dough to a 10 x 16-inch rectangle. Spread 1½ tablespoons margarine over dough; sprinkle sugar mixture and ⅔ cup chocolate chips over dough. Beginning at 1 long edge, roll up tightly. Cut into 1-inch-wide slices and place, cut side down, in a lightly sprayed 8-inch square baking dish. Repeat with remaining ingredients. Lightly spray tops of dough with cooking spray, cover, and let rise in a warm place 1 hour or until almost doubled in size.

Preheat oven to 375 degrees. Bake 18 to 23 minutes. Transfer baking dishes to a wire rack.

For glaze, combine confectioners sugar and water in a small bowl; stir until

smooth. Drizzle over warm rolls; serve warm.

Yield: 32 cinnamon rolls

Served warm from the oven, Chocolate-Cinnamon Rolls are a yummy way to wrap up the party. Made with reduced-fat chocolate chips and margarine, the sweets have half the fat of traditional cinnamon rolls.

1 serving (1 roll): 120 calories, 4.1 grams fat, 1.7 grams protein, 22.4 grams carbohydrate

Gingerbread Party

Like a fairy tale come true, our gingerbread party will have youngsters beaming with excitement and wonder! From the goody-laden tree to the enchanting "gingerbread" house centerpiece, your home will become a dreamland of peppermint swirls, fluffy icing, and sugar-coated gumdrops. Guests will have a sleighload of fun decorating giant gingerbread cookies, stringing candy necklaces, and trimming miniature graham-cracker cottages — while indulging their Yuletide appetites with ice cream punch, sweet snack mix, and more. There are even popcorn treats to take home after the party.

Serve up a tummy-warming beverage that children will love with our yummy Peanut Butter Hot Cocoa. Chocolate-Toffee Bars feature a crunchy candy bar topping on a soft and chewy sugar-cookie crust.

Gingerbread Tree Decorations

Adorned with gingerbread cutouts, colorful gumdrops, and other Yuletide yummies, our small tree is sure to delight party guests. The cute heart, gingerbread man, and star cookie ornaments are made using the Gingerbread Cookies recipe on this page. Ribbon hangers are easily added when you use a drinking straw to cut out a hole in the top of each cookie before baking. Ribbons are also used to hang 1¼" dia. gumdrop rings. A sweet garland of hard candies with holes in the centers and gumdrops is draped among the branches. Purchased candy canes and red and white polka-dot bows made of 1½"w ribbon add the finishing touch to our festive evergreen.

GINGERBREAD COOKIES

COOKIES
- ²/₃ cup butter or margarine, softened
- ¹/₃ cup vegetable shortening
- ³/₄ cup firmly packed brown sugar
- ¹/₂ cup buttermilk
- ¹/₂ cup molasses
- 2 eggs
- 1 teaspoon vanilla extract
- 5¹/₄ cups all-purpose flour
- ¹/₄ cup cocoa
- 2 teaspoons ground cinnamon
- 1¹/₂ teaspoons ground ginger
- 1 teaspoon ground allspice
- 1 teaspoon baking powder
- 1 teaspoon baking soda
- 1 teaspoon salt

ICING
- 1¹/₂ cups sifted confectioners sugar
- 5 teaspoons water
- ¹/₈ teaspoon icing whitener (used in cake decorating)
  Candies to decorate

For cookies, cream butter, shortening, and brown sugar in a large bowl until fluffy. Add buttermilk, molasses, eggs, and vanilla; beat until well blended. In another large bowl, combine remaining ingredients. Add half of dry ingredients to creamed mixture; stir until a soft dough forms. Stir in remaining dry ingredients, 1 cup at a time; use hands if necessary to mix well. Divide dough into fourths. Wrap in plastic wrap and chill 2 hours or until dough is firm.

Preheat oven to 350 degrees. On a lightly floured surface, use a floured rolling pin to roll out one fourth of dough

to slightly less than ¹/₄-inch thickness. Use desired cookie cutters to cut out shapes. Transfer to a greased baking sheet. Bake 7 to 9 minutes or until firm. Transfer cookies to a wire rack to cool. Repeat with remaining dough.

For icing, combine all ingredients in a small bowl; stir until smooth. Spoon icing into a pastry bag fitted with a small round tip. Decorate cookies with icing and desired candies. Allow icing to harden. Store in an airtight container.
Yield: about 1¹/₂ dozen 6-inch cookies **or** about 6¹/₂ dozen 3¹/₄-inch ornament cookies

CHOCOLATE-TOFFEE BARS

- 1 package (18 ounces) refrigerated sugar cookie dough
- 1 cup almond brickle chips
- 1 cup semisweet chocolate chips
- ¹/₂ cup finely chopped pecans

Preheat oven to 350 degrees. Cut cookie dough into large pieces; press into

bottom of a greased 9 x 13-inch baking pan. Sprinkle remaining ingredients evenly over dough. Bake 20 to 25 minutes or until edges are lightly browned. Cool in pan on a wire rack. Cut into 1 x 2-inch bars. Store in an airtight container.
Yield: about 4 dozen bars

PEANUT BUTTER HOT COCOA

- 9 cups milk, divided
- ¹/₂ cup smooth peanut butter
- 1¹/₂ cups chocolate mix for milk
  Whipped cream to garnish

In a Dutch oven, combine 1 cup milk and peanut butter. Stirring frequently, cook over low heat until smooth. Increase heat to medium. Slowly stir in remaining 8 cups milk and chocolate mix. Stirring occasionally, cook just until mixture simmers. Garnish each serving with whipped cream; serve immediately.
Yield: about 9¹/₂ cups cocoa

Mom can bake these delicious Gingerbread Cookies ahead of time (and even decorate a few as a guide for young ones to follow). Children will have a ball giving each large cutout its own sweet personality with icing and candies.

For a taste of Christmas, try refreshing Peppermint Ice Cream Punch. The frothy drink combines vanilla ice cream, crushed hard candies, and a fruit-flavored soft drink. For a spectacular presentation, encircle the base of your bowl with a starry Punch Bowl Cookie Ring. Spicy Baked Taco Dip is loaded with South-of-the-Border flavor, and Ham and Cheese Biscuit Turnovers make tasty appetizers!

Punch Bowl Cookie Ring

For a kid-pleasing presentation, encircle the base of your punch bowl with our cheery cookie ring. The tummy-tempting embellishment is made from our Gingerbread Cookies recipe, page 137, using 2¹/₂"w and 3¹/₂"w star-shaped cookie cutters. (We used one fourth of the dough and one recipe of icing.) The cookies are easily "glued" together with icing to form a circle around the bowl, then decorated with gumdrops, peppermints, and small candy canes.

PEPPERMINT ICE CREAM PUNCH

    1 jar (8 ounces) red maraschino
         cherries, drained
   12 round peppermint candies

---

    2 half-gallons vanilla ice cream,
         softened and divided
    1 cup coarsely crushed peppermint
         candies (about 30 round
         candies), divided
   48 ounces cherry lemon-lime
         soft drink, chilled

Place cherries and peppermint candies in bottom of a 6-cup ring mold. In a large bowl, combine 1 half-gallon ice cream and ¹/₂ cup crushed candies. Spoon ice cream mixture over cherries and candies in mold. Cover and freeze 4 hours or until firm.

In a large bowl, combine remaining half-gallon ice cream and ¹/₂ cup crushed candies; cover and store in freezer.

To serve, spoon peppermint ice cream mixture into punch bowl. Stirring constantly, pour soft drink over ice cream mixture until blended. Dip mold into warm water to loosen ice cream ring. Place ice cream ring in punch.

Yield: about 16 cups punch

BAKED TACO DIP

    1 can (16 ounces) refried beans
   ¹/₂ teaspoon ground cumin
   ¹/₂ teaspoon garlic salt
   ¹/₂ teaspoon onion powder
   ¹/₂ pound lean ground beef
   ¹/₂ cup chopped onion
   ¹/₂ cup taco sauce
  1¹/₂ cups (6 ounces) shredded Cheddar
         cheese
         Tortilla chips to serve

Preheat oven to 350 degrees. In a small bowl, combine beans, cumin, garlic salt, and onion powder. Spread mixture in bottom of a lightly greased 9-inch pie plate. In a small skillet, cook ground beef and onion over medium heat until meat is browned; drain well. Layer meat mixture, taco sauce, and cheese over bean mixture. Bake 25 to 30 minutes or until heated through and cheese is melted. Serve warm with chips.

Yield: about 3¹/₂ cups dip

HAM AND CHEESE BISCUIT TURNOVERS

¹/₃ cup diced ham (about 3¹/₂ ounces)
¹/₃ cup shredded Cheddar cheese
2 tablespoons mayonnaise
1 can (7.5 ounces) refrigerated
    buttermilk biscuits
    Vegetable cooking spray

Preheat oven to 375 degrees. In a small bowl, combine ham, cheese, and mayonnaise. Press each biscuit into a 3-inch-diameter circle. Spoon about 1 tablespoon ham mixture in center of each biscuit and fold over; press edges together. Place on a greased baking sheet. Use scissors to cut slits in tops of turnovers. Bake 12 to 15 minutes or until golden brown. Serve warm.
Yield: 10 turnovers

GABRIEL'S HORNS

²/₃ cup purchased chocolate frosting
3 cups bugle-shaped corn snacks
6 ounces vanilla candy coating
    Multicolored non-pareils to
    decorate

Spoon frosting into a pastry bag fitted with a large round tip. Pipe frosting into each corn snack. In a small microwave-safe bowl, microwave candy coating on high power (100%) 2 minutes or until coating softens, stirring after 1 minute. Stir until smooth. Dip large end of each corn snack into candy coating. Sprinkle non-pareils over candy coating. Place on waxed paper; allow coating to harden. Store in an airtight container.
Yield: about 8 dozen snacks

BACON CHEESE DIP

8 ounces pasteurized process cheese
1 package (8 ounces) cream cheese
¹/₄ cup milk
1 tablespoon Worcestershire sauce
1 teaspoon onion powder
¹/₂ cup crumbled cooked bacon
    Carrot sticks to serve

In a medium saucepan, combine all ingredients except bacon. Stirring frequently, cook over low heat until smooth. Reserving 1 tablespoon bacon for garnish, stir in remaining bacon. Garnish with reserved bacon. Serve warm with carrot sticks.
Yield: about 2¹/₄ cups dip

Easy-to-make Gabriel's Horns are playful party treats. The bugle-shaped corn snacks are filled with chocolate frosting and dipped in vanilla candy coating and colorful sprinkles. Robust Bacon Cheese Dip is great served with veggies. Packed with chewy oats and brown sugar, Chocolate-Peanut Butter Granola Squares hit the spot when youngsters need an energy boost.

CHOCOLATE-PEANUT BUTTER GRANOLA SQUARES

1 package (7 ounces) bran
    muffin mix
¹/₂ cup old-fashioned oats
¹/₄ cup firmly packed brown sugar
¹/₂ cup butter or margarine, softened
¹/₄ cup crunchy peanut butter
¹/₂ cup semisweet chocolate chips

Preheat oven to 325 degrees. In a medium bowl, combine muffin mix, oats, and brown sugar. With a pastry blender or 2 knives, cut in butter and peanut butter until mixture is well blended and crumbly. Stir in chocolate chips. Press into a 7 x 11-inch greased baking pan. Bake 28 to 32 minutes or until golden brown and firm. Cool in pan on a wire rack. Cut into 1¹/₂-inch squares. Store in an airtight container.
Yield: about 2 dozen squares

POPCORN CRUNCH BALLS

- 8 cups popped popcorn
- ¹/₂ cup small red cinnamon candies
- 1 package (10¹/₂ ounces) miniature marshmallows
- 3 tablespoons butter or margarine

Combine popcorn and candies in a large bowl. Place marshmallows and butter in a large saucepan. Stirring frequently, cook over low heat until marshmallows melt. Pour marshmallow mixture over popcorn mixture; stir until well coated. Use greased hands to shape into 2¹/₂-inch balls. Let popcorn cool completely. Store in an airtight container.
Yield: about 8 popcorn balls

CARAMEL APPLE SNACK MIX

- 2¹/₂ cups broken pretzel pieces
- 2¹/₂ cups bite-size square rice cereal
- 2 cups apple-flavored round toasted oat cereal
- ¹/₂ cup sunflower kernels
- 1 package (14 ounces) caramels
- ¹/₄ cup water

Preheat oven to 250 degrees. In a large bowl, combine pretzels, rice cereal, oat cereal, and sunflower kernels. Place caramels and water in a small saucepan. Stirring frequently, cook over low heat until smooth. Pour caramel mixture over cereal mixture; stir until well coated. Spread mixture evenly in a greased 10¹/₂ x 15¹/₂-inch jellyroll pan. Bake 1 hour, stirring every 15 minutes. Spread on greased aluminum foil to cool. Break into pieces. Store in an airtight container.
Yield: about 10 cups snack mix

ORANGE CREAM DIP

- ¹/₂ cup sugar
- ¹/₄ cup orange juice
- 1 egg
- 2 tablespoons all-purpose flour
- 1 cup whipping cream, whipped
  Orange zest strip to garnish
  Fresh orange sections to serve

Combine sugar, orange juice, egg, and flour in a small saucepan. Whisking constantly, cook over medium-low heat about 12 minutes or until mixture thickens. Transfer to a medium bowl; cover and chill.

To serve, fold whipped cream into orange juice mixture. Garnish with orange zest. Serve with orange sections.
Yield: about 2 cups dip

For perfect take-home party favors, treat kids to our cinnamony Popcorn Crunch Balls. Crispy Chicken Wings with Ranch-Style Dip are sure to be snatched up in a flash. Kissed with citrus flavor, Orange Cream Dip is wonderful served with fruit. Nutty Caramel Apple Snack Mix delights the senses with its munchable sweetness.

Small guests can create their own Edible Necklaces using a variety of their favorite candies and small gingerbread cookie cutouts.

CRISPY CHICKEN WINGS WITH RANCH-STYLE DIP

1   package (8 ounces) cream cheese,
      softened
½   cup sour cream
1   envelope (0.4 ounce) ranch-style
      salad dressing mix
2   pounds chicken wings
1   teaspoon salt
1½   cups corn flake crumbs
3   egg whites

In a small bowl, combine cream cheese, sour cream, and salad dressing mix. Cover and chill until ready to serve.

Preheat oven to 375 degrees. Cut off and discard chicken wing tips. Cut chicken wings in half at joint. Sprinkle with salt; set aside. Place cereal crumbs and egg whites in separate small bowls. Beat egg whites until foamy. Dip chicken pieces, 1 at a time, in egg whites and roll in crumbs. Place on a greased baking sheet. Bake 30 to 40 minutes or until

juices run clear when chicken is pierced with a fork. Serve warm with dip.
Yield: 18 to 22 pieces chicken

Edible Necklaces

Children will have fun creating our clever cookie and candy necklaces! To fashion the edible party favors, we used a plastic needle to string gumdrops, wrapped peppermints, and candies with holes in the centers onto thin ribbon. Each necklace is completed by tying a cookie cutout to its center (a drinking straw is used to cut a hole in the top of each cookie before baking). The cookies are made using the Gingerbread Cookies recipe, page 137, and a variety of cookie cutter shapes. What great goodies to wear home and eat later!

Captivate little ones with a magical Centerpiece House made by gluing graham crackers to a box and adding decorations of butter cookies, candies, and royal icing. Upside-down ice-cream cones are transformed into tiny evergreens using swirls of icing, and coconut is sprinkled about for new-fallen snow. So the children can enjoy creating smaller, edible versions of the centerpiece during the party, make a cottage with "snow"-capped eaves ahead of time for each guest to trim with goodies; then provide plenty of gumdrops, chewing gum, wrapped hard candies, peppermint sticks, cinnamon candies, and other purchased sweets.

CENTERPIECE HOUSE

This house is for decoration only.

You will need an empty 6½-inch-wide x 11-inch-long shoe box without a lid, cardboard, Royal Icing (recipe on this page), craft knife, graham crackers (2½ x 5 inches), coconut, pastry bag fitted with a large round tip, hot glue gun, and items to decorate house (we used gumdrops, hard candies, peppermint sticks, small red cinnamon candies, butter-flavored cookies, and sugar wafer cookies).

1. To make front wall of house, draw a 6½-inch-wide x 5-inch-high rectangle on cardboard. Mark center top with a pencil. Refer to **Fig. 1** to draw a line 3 inches high from center mark and then to draw 2 connecting lines to form roof. Cut out shape. Repeat to make back wall. Place shoe box open side up. Glue pieces to each end of shoe box.

Fig. 1

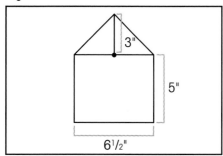

2. To make 1 side wall/roof piece of house, draw an 11-inch-wide x 9½-inch-high rectangle on cardboard. Cut out shape. Refer to **Fig. 2** to draw a line 5 inches from bottom. Use craft knife to score line. Bend cardboard to form roof. Repeat to make second side wall/roof piece. Glue pieces to each side of shoe box and along top of roof.

Fig. 2

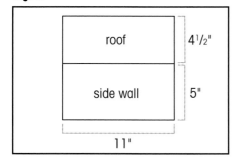

3. (**Note:** Use a serrated knife and a sawing motion to cut graham crackers.) Cut crackers as necessary to fit and hot glue to sides, front, and back of shoe box (do not glue graham crackers to roof).

4. Use pastry bag filled with royal icing to pipe windows onto sides of house and to attach door, shutters, cookies on roof, and candy decorations. Allow icing to harden.

COTTAGES AND TREES

For each cottage, you will need graham cracker halves (2½-inch square), Royal Icing (recipe on this page), white poster board, pastry bag, small and medium round tips, and items to decorate cottage (we used small red cinnamon candies, gumdrops, stick gum, wrapped hard candies, small chocolate bars, and hard ring-shaped candies).

For each tree, you will need 1 cone-shaped sugar ice-cream cone, Royal Icing (recipe on this page) tinted green using green paste food coloring, and pastry bag fitted with medium tip.

1. (**Note:** Use a serrated knife and a sawing motion to cut graham crackers. Use royal icing and a medium tip to attach all cracker pieces and decorations to cottage.) Refer to **Fig. 1** to cut corners from 1 cracker half for front wall of cottage. Repeat for back wall.

Fig. 1

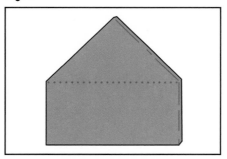

2. Refer to **Fig. 2** to attach front and back walls to 1 cracker half (base). Hold walls upright or use something to prop walls until icing hardens.

Fig. 2

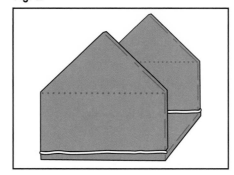

3. For side walls, refer to **Fig. 3** to attach 2 cracker quarters to base and front and back walls. Allow icing to harden.

Fig. 3

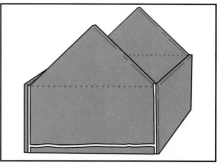

4. For roof, apply icing to top edges of walls. Refer to **Fig. 4** to place 2 cracker halves on top of cottage. Apply icing along peak of roof. Allow icing to harden.

Fig. 4

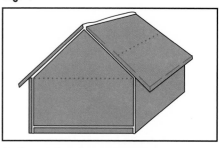

5. For yard, cut an irregularly shaped 6 x 7-inch piece from poster board. Use icing to attach cottage to poster board. Pipe snow onto roof.

6. Attach candies and other items to cottage for decorations. Decorate yard with sidewalk and shrubs.

7. Use small round tip to pipe icicles onto cottage and snow onto yard decorations. Allow icing to harden. Spread icing on poster board. Sprinkle yard with coconut; press into icing.

8. For tree, pipe swirls of green royal icing onto inverted ice-cream cones. Allow icing to harden.

ROYAL ICING

   5 cups sifted confectioners sugar
   7 tablespoons warm water
   3 tablespoons plus 1 teaspoon meringue powder
   ½ teaspoon lemon extract

Beat confectioners sugar, water, meringue powder, and lemon extract in a medium bowl with an electric mixer 7 to 10 minutes or until stiff. Spoon icing into a pastry bag fitted with desired tip.
Yield: about 3¼ cups icing (will decorate centerpiece house, **or** 5 cottages, **or** 12 trees)

WHITE CHRISTMAS DREAMS

While Jack Frost transforms the landscape into a magical snow scene, you can do the same indoors with a menu inspired by the wintry fellow's handiwork! Our elegantly dressed table is laden with a flurry of dreamy white desserts. Indulge holiday guests with luscious offerings that'll capture their attention as well as their appetites, from our chocolaty Yule log to chewy nougat squares!

Featuring a whipped filling flavored with crème de cacao and white baking chocolate, our White Chocolate Yule Log is so delicious that not even a crumb will be left! The iced cake is dusted with confectioners sugar and edible glitter "snow" for an enchanting finish.

WHITE CHOCOLATE YULE LOG

CAKE
- 5 eggs, separated
- 2/3 cup granulated sugar, divided
- 2 tablespoons butter or margarine, melted
- 1 1/2 teaspoons vanilla extract
- 3/4 cup sifted cake flour
- 1 1/4 teaspoons baking powder
- 1/4 teaspoon salt
- 2 tablespoons sifted confectioners sugar

FILLING
- 3 tablespoons butter
- 1 egg yolk
- 2/3 cup plus 1 tablespoon whipping cream, divided
- 1 tablespoon white crème de cacao
- 1 ounce white baking chocolate
- 1 tablespoon sifted confectioners sugar

ICING
- 1/4 cup milk
- 2 ounces white baking chocolate
- 1 teaspoon vanilla extract
- 3/4 cup chilled butter, cut into pieces
- 1 cup sifted confectioners sugar
  Confectioners sugar, white edible glitter, bows, and artificial decorations to decorate

Preheat oven to 350 degrees. For cake, grease a 10 1/2 x 15 1/2-inch jellyroll pan. Line bottom of pan with waxed paper; grease waxed paper. In a large bowl, beat egg yolks until thick. Add 1/3 cup granulated sugar; beat until well blended. Beat in melted butter and vanilla. In another large bowl, beat egg whites until foamy. Gradually add remaining 1/3 cup granulated sugar; beat until stiff peaks form. Fold egg white mixture into egg yolk mixture. In a small bowl, combine cake flour, baking powder, and salt. Sift about one-fourth of flour mixture at a time over egg mixture, folding in flour after each addition until mixture is well blended. Pour batter into prepared pan. Bake 11 to 14 minutes or until toothpick inserted in center of cake comes out clean. Sift confectioners sugar onto a towel. Loosen edges of cake and immediately invert onto towel. Remove waxed paper from cake. Beginning with 1 long edge, roll cake in towel and allow to cool.

For filling, combine butter, egg yolk, and 1 tablespoon whipping cream in a heavy small saucepan. Stirring constantly, cook over low heat about 8 minutes or until mixture thickens.

Loaded with sweetened coconut, a yummy filling tops a flaky homemade crust to make our Coconut Christmas Pie.

Remove from heat. Stir in crème de cacao and white chocolate; stir until chocolate melts. Transfer chocolate mixture to a medium bowl; cool about 30 minutes.

In another medium bowl, beat remaining 2/3 cup whipping cream until soft peaks form. Add confectioners sugar; beat until stiff peaks form. Fold into chocolate mixture. Unroll cake and spread filling over cake. Roll up cake. Place on a serving plate; cover and chill while making icing.

For icing, place milk and white chocolate in a small microwave-safe bowl. Microwave on medium power (50%) 1 1/2 minutes or until chocolate softens, stirring every 30 seconds. Stir until chocolate melts. Stir in vanilla. Cool 30 minutes or until chocolate mixture reaches room temperature.

In a medium bowl, beat butter and confectioners sugar until smooth and creamy. Gradually add chocolate mixture; beat until well blended. Cut a 1-inch slice from one end of cake roll. Place on top of "log" to form "knot." Spread icing over cake roll. Chill cake 5 minutes to let icing harden slightly. Use tines of a fork to form "bark" lines in icing. Sift confectioners sugar and sprinkle glitter over cake for "snow." Decorate cake with bows and artificial decorations.
Yield: about 16 servings

COCONUT CHRISTMAS PIE

CRUST
- 1 1/2 cups all-purpose flour
- 1/2 teaspoon salt
- 1/2 cup vegetable shortening
- 3 to 4 tablespoons cold water

FILLING
- 1 cup sugar, divided
- 1/4 cup all-purpose flour
- 1 envelope unflavored gelatin
- 1/2 teaspoon salt
- 1 can (8.5 ounces) cream of coconut
- 1 cup milk
- 1 cup grated sweetened frozen coconut, divided
- 1 tablespoon clear vanilla extract
- 3 egg whites
- 1 tablespoon water
- 1/4 teaspoon cream of tartar
- 1/2 cup whipping cream, whipped

Preheat oven to 450 degrees. For crust, combine flour and salt in a small bowl. Using a pastry blender or 2 knives, cut in shortening until mixture resembles coarse meal. Sprinkle with water; mix until a soft dough forms. On a lightly floured surface, use a floured rolling pin to roll out dough to 1/8-inch thickness. Transfer to a 9-inch pie plate and use a sharp knife to trim edge of dough. Flute edge of crust. Prick bottom of crust with a fork. Bake 10 to

Continued on page 146

For a simple yet elegant dessert, try Meringue Snowballs in Custard. The poached meringue dollops are served in a sauce of creamy vanilla custard.

12 minutes or until lightly browned. Cool on a wire rack.

For filling, combine ¹/₂ cup sugar, flour, gelatin, and salt in a heavy medium saucepan; stir until well blended. Whisk in cream of coconut and milk. Whisking constantly, cook over medium heat until mixture boils; boil 2 minutes. Transfer mixture to a heatproof medium bowl. Set bowl in a larger bowl containing ice water. Stirring mixture frequently, let cool 15 minutes.

Stir ¹/₂ cup coconut and vanilla into filling. Place egg whites, remaining ¹/₂ cup sugar, water, and cream of tartar in the top of a double boiler over simmering water. Whisking constantly, cook egg whites until a thermometer registers 160 degrees, about 10 minutes. Transfer egg whites to a large bowl; beat until soft peaks form. Fold beaten egg whites and whipped cream into filling. Spoon filling into pie shell. Sprinkle remaining ¹/₂ cup coconut over pie filling. Cover and chill 2 hours or until pie is firm.
Yield: about 8 servings

146

MERINGUE SNOWBALLS IN CUSTARD

- 6 egg yolks
- ²/₃ cup plus ¹/₄ cup sugar, divided
- 6¹/₄ cups milk, divided
- 1¹/₂ teaspoons vanilla extract
- 2 egg whites
- ¹/₄ teaspoon cream of tartar

In a small bowl, beat egg yolks and ²/₃ cup sugar until well blended. Combine egg yolk mixture and 4 cups milk in the top of a double boiler over simmering water. Stirring constantly, cook about 30 minutes or until mixture coats the back of a spoon. Stir in vanilla. Pour custard into a 9 x 13-inch serving dish. Place plastic wrap directly on surface of custard; chill.

Place remaining 2¹/₄ cups milk in a heavy large skillet over medium-low heat. In a medium bowl, beat egg whites until foamy. Gradually add remaining ¹/₄ cup sugar and cream of tartar; beat until stiff peaks form. When milk is almost to a

simmer, use 2 spoons to form and drop rounded tablespoonfuls of meringue into milk. Poach meringues about 4 minutes, turning once during cooking (meringues should be firm to touch). With a slotted spoon, remove meringues from milk; transfer to paper towels to drain. Place meringues on custard. Chill completely before serving.
Yield: about 12 servings

TOASTED PECAN NOUGAT

Use a heavy-duty mixer to make this candy.

- 1 tablespoon plus 1 teaspoon cornstarch, divided
- 1¹/₂ cups sugar
- 1 cup light corn syrup
- ¹/₂ cup water
- ¹/₈ teaspoon salt
- 2 egg whites

1/8 teaspoon cream of tartar
1 teaspoon vanilla extract
1 teaspoon almond extract
1 cup chopped pecans, toasted

Line a 9-inch square baking pan with aluminum foil, extending foil over 2 sides of pan. Grease foil and sprinkle with 1 teaspoon cornstarch. In a heavy large saucepan, combine sugar and remaining 1 tablespoon cornstarch; stir in corn syrup, water, and salt. Stirring constantly, cook over medium-low heat until sugar dissolves. Using a pastry brush dipped in hot water, wash down any sugar crystals on sides of pan. Attach a candy thermometer to pan, making sure thermometer does not touch bottom of pan. Increase heat to medium and bring to a boil. While mixture is boiling, beat egg whites and cream of tartar in a medium bowl until stiff; set aside. Cook sugar mixture, without stirring, until mixture reaches 286 degrees. While beating at high speed, slowly pour hot mixture over egg white mixture. Beat in extracts. Continue to beat until candy begins to hold its shape and lose its gloss. Stir in pecans. Press mixture into pan. Use a wet knife to score warm nougat into 1-inch squares. Allow to cool.

Use ends of foil to lift nougat from pan. Use a serrated knife and a sawing motion to cut into squares. Place each nougat piece in a candy cup and store in an airtight container in refrigerator.
Yield: about 6 dozen pieces nougat

PAVLOVA WITH STRAWBERRY-ORANGE SAUCE

MERINGUE
4 egg whites
1 teaspoon vinegar
1 teaspoon vanilla extract
1/4 teaspoon cream of tartar
1/4 teaspoon salt
1 cup sugar

SAUCE
2 tablespoons cornstarch
1/4 cup orange juice
1 jar (12 ounces) strawberry preserves
1 package (10 ounces) frozen sweetened sliced strawberries, thawed
1/4 cup sugar plus 2 tablespoons sugar, divided
1 1/4 teaspoons grated orange zest
1/2 teaspoon salt
1 cup whipping cream

Pavlova with Strawberry-Orange Sauce *(top)* is a sumptuous creation. Whipped cream is spooned into a meringue "bowl" and topped with a fruity sauce for this famous Australian dessert. Toasted Pecan Nougat is a sweet, chewy confection that's sure to please. Each square is packed with crunchy chopped nuts.

Preheat oven to 250 degrees. For meringue, draw a 9-inch-diameter circle on bottom side of parchment paper. Place paper on a baking sheet. In a medium bowl, beat egg whites, vinegar, vanilla, cream of tartar, and salt until soft peaks form. Gradually add sugar; beat until stiff peaks form. Spoon egg white mixture into circle. With back of spoon, make a slight hollow in center of mixture to hold whipped cream and sauce. Bake 1 1/2 hours. Carefully transfer parchment paper and warm meringue to a wire rack to cool completely (cracks may form).

For sauce, dissolve cornstarch in orange juice in a small bowl. In a medium saucepan over medium heat, combine strawberry preserves, strawberries, 1/4 cup sugar, orange zest, and salt. Cook 3 minutes or until preserves melt and sugar dissolves. Stir in cornstarch mixture. Stirring constantly, increase heat to medium-high; cook 3 minutes or until mixture thickens. Remove from heat and chill 1 1/2 hours.

To serve, beat whipping cream in a medium bowl until soft peaks form. Add remaining 2 tablespoons sugar; beat until stiff peaks form. Spoon whipped cream onto meringue. Spoon sauce over whipped cream. Serve immediately.
Yield: about 8 servings

COFFEEHOUSE SAMPLER

Bring a touch of coffeehouse charm to your Christmas gatherings with our sumptuous sampling of robust coffee drinks and desserts. Guests will enjoy sipping piping hot or iced java and eating delicious treats such as scones, biscotti, cookies, and cakes. You'll brew up the best holiday season ever with these gourmet offerings!

Scrumptiously rich Fudge Brownie Cake is three chocolaty, nutty layers enhanced with a yummy frosting and sweetened whipped cream. Whether served hot or cold, easy-to-make Raspberry Coffee is a sweet indulgence.

FUDGE BROWNIE CAKE

CAKE
1½ cups butter or margarine
6 ounces unsweetened baking
   chocolate
6 eggs
1½ teaspoons vanilla extract
3 cups sugar
1¾ cups all-purpose flour
2 cups chopped pecans

ICING
3½ cups plus 4 tablespoons sifted
   confectioners sugar, divided
½ cup butter or margarine
6 tablespoons milk
3 tablespoons cocoa
1 teaspoon vanilla extract
1 cup finely chopped pecans
2 cups whipping cream
   Chocolate curls to garnish

Preheat oven to 325 degrees. For cake, grease three 8-inch round cake pans. Line bottoms of pans with waxed paper; grease waxed paper. Place butter and chocolate in the top of a double boiler over simmering water. Stirring frequently, heat just until mixture melts. Remove from heat. In a large bowl, beat eggs and vanilla until blended. Stirring constantly, gradually add melted chocolate mixture to egg mixture. In a medium bowl, combine sugar and flour. Gradually stir dry ingredients into chocolate mixture just until blended. Stir in pecans. Spread batter into prepared pans. Bake 25 to 30 minutes or until cake is firm to touch. Cool in pans on a wire rack.

For icing, place 3½ cups confectioners sugar in a large bowl. In a heavy small saucepan, combine butter, milk, and cocoa. Stirring constantly, cook over medium heat until butter melts. Remove from heat; stir in vanilla. Pour chocolate mixture over confectioners sugar; stir until smooth. Stir in pecans. Let icing cool about 15 minutes or until firm enough to spread. Spread icing between layers and on top of cake.

Place whipping cream in a medium bowl. Beat until soft peaks form. Gradually add remaining 4 tablespoons confectioners sugar; beat until stiff peaks form. Ice sides and top edge of cake with whipped cream. Store in an airtight container in refrigerator. To serve, garnish with chocolate curls.
Yield: about 16 servings

Melt-in-your-mouth morsels, Almond Rosettes are piped swirls kissed with almond flavoring. Whipping cream and ice cream give liqueur-laced Creamy Coffee Punch its wonderful frothiness.

RASPBERRY COFFEE

1 cup half and half
⅔ cup sugar
1 quart hot, strongly brewed
   raspberry-flavored coffee

For hot coffee, place half and half and sugar in a small saucepan over medium-low heat. Stirring frequently, heat about 10 minutes or until hot. Combine coffee and half and half mixture in a 1½-quart heatproof container; serve hot.

For iced coffee, combine coffee and sugar in a 1½-quart heatproof container. Stir until sugar dissolves; cover and chill. To serve, stir half and half into coffee mixture; serve over ice.
Yield: about 5 cups coffee

CREAMY COFFEE PUNCH

2 quarts hot, strongly brewed coffee
3 tablespoons sugar
2 teaspoons vanilla extract
2 cups coffee-flavored liqueur
1 quart vanilla ice cream, softened
2 cups whipping cream, whipped

Place coffee in a 3-quart heatproof container. Add sugar and vanilla; stir until sugar dissolves. Allow mixture to cool. Stir in liqueur; cover and chill.

To serve, pour chilled coffee mixture into a punch bowl. Stir in ice cream. Fold in whipped cream. Serve immediately.
Yield: about 16 cups punch

ALMOND ROSETTES

1 cup butter or margarine, softened
1 cup sugar
1 egg
3 tablespoons milk
1 teaspoon almond extract
2½ cups all-purpose flour
1 teaspoon baking powder
   Sliced almonds to decorate

Preheat oven to 350 degrees. In a large bowl, cream butter and sugar until fluffy. Add egg, milk, and almond extract; beat until smooth. In a medium bowl, combine flour and baking powder. Add dry ingredients to creamed mixture; stir until a soft dough forms. Transfer about one-third of dough into a pastry bag fitted with a large open star tip. Pipe 2-inch-diameter rosettes onto a lightly greased baking sheet. Press an almond slice in center of each cookie. Bake 8 to 11 minutes or until bottoms are lightly browned. Transfer cookies to a wire rack to cool. Repeat with remaining dough. Store in an airtight container.
Yield: about 3½ dozen cookies

MAPLE-PECAN COOKIES

- ³/₄ cup butter or margarine, softened
- 1 cup firmly packed brown sugar
- 1 egg
- ¹/₄ cup maple syrup
- 1 teaspoon vanilla extract
- ¹/₄ teaspoon orange extract
- 1 cup all-purpose flour
- ¹/₂ teaspoon baking powder
- 1¹/₄ cups finely chopped pecans, toasted
- ¹/₂ cup quick-cooking oats

Preheat oven to 375 degrees. In a large bowl, cream butter and brown sugar until fluffy. Add egg, maple syrup, and extracts; beat until well blended. In a small bowl, combine flour and baking powder. Add dry ingredients to creamed mixture; stir until a soft dough forms. Stir in pecans and oats. Drop teaspoonfuls of dough 2 inches apart on an ungreased baking sheet. Bake 7 to 9 minutes or until edges are lightly browned. Cool cookies on baking sheet 2 minutes; transfer to a wire rack to cool completely. Store in an airtight container.
Yield: about 5 dozen cookies

OATMEAL-WALNUT SCONES

- 1 cup all-purpose flour
- ²/₃ cup whole-wheat flour
- ¹/₃ cup sugar
- 1¹/₂ teaspoons baking powder
- ³/₄ teaspoon baking soda
- ¹/₄ teaspoon salt
- ³/₄ cup chilled butter or margarine, cut into small pieces
- 1¹/₄ cups quick-cooking oats
- ³/₄ cup finely chopped walnuts, toasted
- ³/₄ cup buttermilk
- ¹/₂ teaspoon vanilla extract
- 1 egg, lightly beaten

Preheat oven to 350 degrees. Combine flours, sugar, baking powder, baking soda, and salt in a large bowl. Using a pastry blender or 2 knives, cut in butter until mixture resembles fine meal. Stir in oats and walnuts. Add buttermilk and vanilla; stir just until mixture is blended. On a lightly floured surface, pat dough to ¹/₂-inch thickness. Use a 3-inch-diameter cookie cutter dipped in flour to cut out scones. Place 1 inch apart on a lightly greased baking sheet. Brush tops of scones with beaten egg. Bake 18 to 22 minutes or until scones are lightly browned. Serve warm.
Yield: about 15 scones

This delightful sampling features coffee-shop favorites, including hearty Oatmeal-Walnut Scones *(clockwise from top left)*, chewy Maple-Pecan Cookies, and a twice-baked Italian specialty — Chocolate-Almond Biscotti.

CHOCOLATE-ALMOND BISCOTTI

- ¹/₂ cup butter or margarine, softened
- ¹/₂ cup firmly packed brown sugar
- ¹/₂ cup granulated sugar
- 3 eggs
- 1 teaspoon almond extract
- 2¹/₂ cups all-purpose flour
- 1 teaspoon baking powder
- ¹/₂ teaspoon baking soda
- ¹/₈ teaspoon salt
- 1 cup semisweet chocolate mini chips
- 1 cup coarsely ground almonds, toasted

Preheat oven to 375 degrees. In a large bowl, cream butter and sugars until fluffy. Add eggs and almond extract; beat until smooth. In a medium bowl, combine flour, baking powder, baking soda, and salt. Add dry ingredients to creamed mixture; stir until a soft dough forms. Stir in chocolate chips and almonds. Divide dough in half. On a greased and floured baking sheet, shape each piece of dough into a 2¹/₂ x 10-inch loaf, flouring hands as necessary. Allow 3 inches between loaves on baking sheet. Bake 20 to 24 minutes or until loaves are firm and lightly browned; cool 10 minutes on baking sheet.

Cut loaves diagonally into ¹/₂-inch slices. Lay slices flat on an ungreased baking sheet. Bake 5 to 7 minutes; turn slices over and bake 5 to 7 minutes longer or until golden brown. Transfer cookies to a wire rack to cool. Store in a cookie tin.
Yield: about 3 dozen cookies

A buttery brown sugar and banana mixture and a cinnamon streusel topping are baked right on top of Banana Crumb Cake for a moist treat. Guests will love pairing the cake with Caramel Mocha — a rich, smooth dessert beverage flavored with caramel ice cream topping and chocolate syrup.

BANANA CRUMB CAKE

BANANA TOPPING
- ½ cup firmly packed brown sugar
- 2 teaspoons cornstarch
- ½ cup water
- 2 tablespoons butter or margarine
- 2 bananas, sliced

CRUMB MIXTURE
- 1 cup all-purpose flour
- ⅔ cup firmly packed brown sugar
- ¾ teaspoon ground cinnamon
- ½ cup chilled butter or margarine

CAKE
- ¾ cup butter or margarine, softened
- 1¼ cups sugar
- 2 eggs
- 2 teaspoons vanilla extract
- 2 cups all-purpose flour
- 1 teaspoon baking powder
- ½ teaspoon baking soda
- ¾ cup buttermilk

For banana topping, combine brown sugar and cornstarch in a heavy small saucepan. Stirring constantly over medium-high heat, gradually add water. Bring mixture to a boil; cook about 1 minute or until mixture begins to thicken. Add butter; stir until butter melts. Remove from heat. Stir in banana slices; set aside.

For crumb mixture, combine flour, brown sugar, and cinnamon in a medium bowl. With a pastry blender or 2 forks, cut in butter until mixture resembles very coarse crumbs; set aside.

Preheat oven to 350 degrees. For cake, cream butter and sugar in a large bowl until fluffy. Add eggs; beat until smooth. Stir in vanilla. In a medium bowl, combine flour, baking powder, and baking soda. Alternately add dry ingredients and buttermilk to creamed mixture; beat until well blended. Spread batter in a greased 10-inch springform pan. Spoon banana topping over batter. Sprinkle crumb mixture over topping. Bake 50 to 60 minutes or until top is golden brown and a toothpick inserted in center of cake comes out clean. Cool cake in pan 30 minutes. Remove sides of pan; serve warm.
Yield: about 12 servings

CARAMEL MOCHA

- 1 can (14 ounces) sweetened condensed milk
- 1 container (12 ounces) caramel ice cream topping
- ½ cup chocolate-flavored syrup
- 2½ quarts hot, strongly brewed coffee (we used espresso roast coffee)

In a small Dutch oven, combine sweetened condensed milk, caramel topping, and chocolate syrup. Stirring constantly, cook over medium-low heat about 8 minutes or until mixture is well blended and hot. Add coffee; stir until blended. Serve hot.
Yield: about 12 cups coffee

STOCKING STUFFERS

Playing Santa has never been easier than with this collection of delicious gift-giving ideas! Impress the boss, a favorite teacher, or a special co-worker with decadent chocolate candies, sweet cookies, spirited cakes, and so much more — all presented in imaginatively trimmed stockings to suit each person's personality and style.

Macadamia Nut Candied Corn is a crunchy gourmet treat perfect for satisfying the munchies. We delivered ours in a plain stocking embellished with buttons, a multi-loop bow, and silk greenery. Laden with toasted pecans and coconut, German Chocolate Fudge is a rich, dark confection that's sure to be savored. Small boxes of the sweets are tied with raffia and tucked inside a gingham stocking trimmed with little wooden hearts.

MACADAMIA NUT CANDIED CORN

24 cups popped popcorn
2 cups macadamia nuts
1³/₄ cups sugar
1 cup butter or margarine
¹/₂ cup light corn syrup
¹/₂ teaspoon salt
3 cups miniature marshmallows
¹/₄ teaspoon butter flavoring

Preheat oven to 250 degrees. Place popcorn and macadamia nuts in a greased large roasting pan. In a heavy large saucepan, combine sugar, butter, corn syrup, and salt over medium heat. Stirring constantly, bring to a boil. Boil 2 minutes without stirring. Remove from heat. Add marshmallows; stir until melted. Stir in butter flavoring. Pour marshmallow mixture over popcorn mixture; stir until well coated. Bake 1 hour, stir every 15 minutes. Spread on lightly greased aluminum foil to cool. Store in an airtight container.
Yield: about 26 cups candied corn

GERMAN CHOCOLATE FUDGE

4 packages (4 ounces each) German baking chocolate, chopped
1 can (14 ounces) sweetened condensed milk
1 cup chopped pecans, toasted
1 cup flaked coconut
2 teaspoons vanilla extract

Line an 8-inch square baking pan with aluminum foil, extending foil over 2 sides of pan; grease foil. Combine chocolate and sweetened condensed milk in a large microwave-safe bowl. Microwave on high power (100%) 2 minutes or until chocolate softens, stirring after each minute. Stir mixture until chocolate melts. Stir in pecans, coconut, and vanilla. Spread mixture into prepared pan. Cover and chill 2 hours or until firm. Cut into 1-inch squares. Store in an airtight container in a cool place.
Yield: about 4 dozen pieces fudge

BRANDIED FRUITCAKE

1 cup chopped dried apricots
1 cup golden raisins
¹/₄ cup orange-flavored liqueur
2 cups butter
2 cups sugar
6 eggs
¹/₂ cup brandy
1 teaspoon vanilla extract

Chock-full of candied fruits and chopped nuts, Brandied Fruitcake is a spirited version of the traditional holiday favorite. The loaf is packed inside a simple stocking decked with fused-on fabric hearts and a sweet sentiment written with a permanent pen.

4 cups all-purpose flour, divided
2 teaspoons baking powder
1 teaspoon ground cinnamon
1 teaspoon ground allspice
¹/₂ teaspoon salt
3 cups chopped pecans
1 cup chopped candied orange peel
1 cup chopped candied pineapple
1 cup candied red cherry halves
1 cup candied green cherry halves
3 tablespoons light corn syrup
1 tablespoon hot water
Pecan halves and candied red and green cherry halves to decorate
Brandy

In a medium bowl, combine apricots, raisins, and liqueur. Allow to stand 2 hours, stirring occasionally.
Preheat oven to 325 degrees. Line four 4¹/₂ x 8¹/₂-inch loaf pans with waxed paper; grease waxed paper. In a very large bowl, cream butter and sugar until fluffy. Add eggs; beat until smooth. Stir in brandy and vanilla. In a medium bowl, combine 3 cups flour, baking powder, cinnamon, allspice, and salt. Add dry ingredients to creamed mixture; beat until well blended.

In a large bowl, combine pecans, orange peel, pineapple, and cherry halves. Stir in remaining 1 cup flour; stir until fruit is coated. Add both fruit mixtures to cake batter; stir until well blended. Spoon batter into prepared pans. Bake 40 minutes. Remove from oven. Combine corn syrup and hot water in a small bowl. Brush corn syrup mixture over top of each loaf. Decorate each loaf with pecans and candied cherry halves. Brush again with corn syrup mixture. Bake 5 minutes longer or until a toothpick inserted in center of cake comes out clean. If cake begins to brown too much, lightly cover with aluminum foil. Cool in pans 15 minutes. Remove from pans and cool completely on a wire rack. Wrap each loaf in a large piece of brandy-soaked cheesecloth, then in heavy-duty aluminum foil. Loaves can be eaten at this time or drizzled with 2 tablespoons brandy once a week for 4 weeks. Store in a cool place.
Yield: 4 fruitcakes

Resembling delicate porcelain china, our tasty Teacup Cookies are decorated with glaze and piped icing. The sweets are individually wrapped in cellophane and romantically presented in a Battenberg lace stocking embellished with a silk rose, ivy, and a wired-ribbon bow.

TEACUP COOKIES

COOKIES
- ³/₄ cup butter or margarine, softened
- ¹/₂ cup granulated sugar
- ¹/₂ cup sifted confectioners sugar
- 1 egg
- 1 teaspoon almond extract
- ¹/₂ teaspoon vanilla extract
- 2 cups all-purpose flour
- ¹/₈ teaspoon salt

DECORATING ICING
- 2¹/₂ cups sifted confectioners sugar
- 2¹/₂ to 3 tablespoons water
- ¹/₂ teaspoon almond extract
  Blue, green, and pink paste food coloring

GLAZE
- 2¹/₂ cups sifted confectioners sugar
- 2¹/₂ to 3 tablespoons water
- 1 teaspoon almond extract

Preheat oven to 350 degrees. Trace teacup pattern onto clear acetate; cut out. For cookies, cream butter and sugars in a medium bowl until fluffy. Add egg and extracts; beat until smooth. In a small bowl, combine flour and salt. Add dry ingredients to creamed mixture; stir until a soft dough forms. On a lightly floured surface, use a floured rolling pin to roll out dough to ¹/₈-inch thickness. Place pattern on dough and use a sharp knife to cut out cookies. Transfer to a greased baking sheet. Bake 8 to 10 minutes or until bottoms are lightly browned. Transfer cookies to a wire rack to cool.

For decorating icing, combine confectioners sugar, water, and almond extract in a small bowl; stir until smooth. Divide icing into 3 small bowls; tint pastel blue, green, and pink. Spoon icing into pastry bags fitted with small round tips.

Pipe outline of teacup onto each cookie. Allow icing to harden. Reserve remaining icing.

For glaze, combine confectioners sugar, water, and almond extract in a small bowl; stir until smooth (icing should be thin enough to flow easily). Spoon glaze into a pastry bag fitted with a round tip. Pipe glaze onto cookie, filling in outline. Allow glaze to harden.

Pipe designs on glaze using remaining decorating icing. Allow icing to harden. Store in a single layer in an airtight container.

Yield: about 2 dozen cookies

CHOCOLATE-DIPPED FRUIT AND NUT CANDIES

3/4 cup chopped dried apricots
3/4 cup chopped dates
3/4 cup chopped walnuts
1/2 cup flaked coconut
1/4 cup butter or margarine, softened
1/4 cup light corn syrup
1/2 teaspoon vanilla extract
3 cups sifted confectioners sugar
8 ounces chocolate candy coating
4 ounces semisweet baking chocolate

Process apricots, dates, walnuts, and coconut in a food processor until coarsely chopped. In a medium bowl, cream butter and corn syrup until fluffy. Stir in vanilla. Beating with an electric mixer, gradually add confectioners sugar to butter mixture until too stiff to beat. Stir in remaining sugar. Pour mixture onto a dampened smooth surface. Knead until very smooth and creamy. Knead in fruit mixture. Shape rounded teaspoonfuls of candy into balls. Place on waxed paper. Loosely cover with waxed paper and allow to dry overnight at room temperature.

Stirring frequently, melt candy coating and baking chocolate in a heavy small saucepan over low heat. Remove from heat (if chocolate mixture begins to harden, return to heat). Dip each candy into chocolate. Place on a baking sheet lined with waxed paper. Use a fork dipped in remaining chocolate to swirl over candies. Chill until firm. Store in an airtight container in a cool place.
Yield: about 4 1/2 dozen candies

CRANBERRY-ORANGE FUDGE

1 cup sweetened dried cranberries
2 tablespoons orange juice
2 cups sugar
1 cup whipping cream
1 tablespoon light corn syrup
2 tablespoons butter or margarine
1 teaspoon vanilla extract
1/2 cup finely chopped candied orange peel

Combine cranberries and orange juice in a small microwave-safe bowl. Cover and microwave on high power (100%) 2 minutes, stirring after 1 minute. Allow covered cranberry mixture to stand 10 minutes. Pulse process mixture in a food processor until coarsely chopped.

Line an 8-inch square baking pan with aluminum foil, extending foil over 2 sides of pan; grease foil. Butter sides of a heavy

Chocolate-Dipped Fruit and Nut Candies and Cranberry-Orange Fudge are two luscious goodies that connoisseurs of confections will love! Present your offerings in an elegant stocking adorned with starry appliqués, a golden tassel, and other opulent trims.

large saucepan. Combine sugar, whipping cream, and corn syrup. Stirring constantly, cook over medium-low heat until sugar dissolves. Using a pastry brush dipped in hot water, wash down any sugar crystals on sides of pan. Attach a candy thermometer to pan, making sure thermometer does not touch bottom of pan. Increase heat to medium and bring to a boil. Cook, without stirring, until mixture reaches soft-ball stage (approximately 234 to 240 degrees). Test about 1/2 teaspoon mixture in ice water. Mixture will easily form a ball in

ice water but will flatten when held in your hand. Place pan in 2 inches of cold water in sink. Add butter and vanilla; do not stir. Cool to approximately 110 degrees. Remove from sink. Using medium speed of an electric mixer, beat until fudge thickens and begins to lose its gloss. Stir in orange peel and cranberries. Pour into prepared pan. Cover and chill 2 hours or until firm.

Cut into 1-inch squares, wiping knife clean between cuts. Store in an airtight container in refrigerator.
Yield: about 4 dozen pieces fudge

A wonderful gift for the young at heart, bejeweled stockings personalized with dimensional glitter paint are packed with everything needed to make delicious, buttery sugar cookies. Our Christmas Cookie Kits include cookie mix, a cookie cutter, baking instructions, and decorating sugars. You'll want to tuck in samples of the baked treats, too.

CHRISTMAS COOKIE KITS

1 cup butter or margarine, softened
1/2 cup vegetable shortening
5 cups all-purpose flour
2 1/2 cups granulated sugar
1 cup firmly packed brown sugar
2 teaspoons baking powder
1 teaspoon salt
  Cookie cutters and red and green decorating sugars to give with mixes

In a small bowl, beat butter and shortening until fluffy. In a large bowl, combine flour, granulated sugar, brown sugar, baking powder, and salt. Using a pastry blender or 2 knives, cut butter mixture into dry ingredients until mixture resembles coarse meal. Divide cookie mix in half and place in 2 resealable plastic bags. Store in refrigerator. Give each mix with a 3-inch-wide star-shaped cookie cutter, decorating sugars, and recipe for Christmas Cookies.
Yield: about 11 1/2 cups cookie mix

CHRISTMAS COOKIES
1 bag (about 5 3/4 cups) Cookie Mix
1 egg
1/4 cup water
1 teaspoon vanilla extract

Preheat oven to 375 degrees. In a large bowl, combine cookie mix, egg, water, and vanilla; stir until a soft dough forms. On a lightly floured surface, use a floured rolling pin to roll out dough to 1/4-inch thickness. Use cookie cutter to cut out cookies. Transfer to a greased baking sheet. Sprinkle cookies with decorating sugar. Bake 6 to 8 minutes or until bottoms are lightly browned. Transfer cookies to a wire rack to cool. Store in an airtight container.
Yield: about 3 1/2 dozen cookies

CANDIED APPLE BUTTER

6 cups applesauce
3 cups firmly packed brown sugar
1/2 cup small red cinnamon candies
1 teaspoon ground cinnamon
1/4 teaspoon ground allspice

Combine applesauce, brown sugar, candies, cinnamon, and allspice in a heavy Dutch oven. Stirring constantly, cook over medium heat until candies melt and sugar dissolves. Reduce heat to medium-low. Stirring occasionally, simmer uncovered about 40 minutes or until mixture thickens. Cool and store in an airtight container in refrigerator.
Yield: about 6½ cups apple butter

CINNAMON-CARROT BREAD

BREAD
3/4 cup coarsely crushed cinnamon graham crackers (about five 2½ x 5-inch crackers)
3/4 cup chopped pecans
1 cup sugar
3/4 cup vegetable oil
2 eggs
1/2 teaspoon orange extract
1 cup shredded carrots
1 1/3 cups all-purpose flour
1 teaspoon ground cinnamon
1/2 teaspoon salt
1/2 teaspoon baking powder

ICING
3/4 cup sifted confectioners sugar
1 tablespoon water
1/2 teaspoon orange extract

Preheat oven to 350 degrees. For bread, grease four 2½ x 5-inch loaf pans. Line pans with waxed paper; grease waxed paper. In a medium bowl, combine cracker crumbs and pecans; set aside. In a large bowl, combine sugar, oil, eggs, and orange extract; beat until blended. Stir in carrots. In a small bowl, combine flour, cinnamon, salt, and baking powder. Add dry ingredients to oil mixture; stir just until moistened. Spoon half of batter into prepared pans. Sprinkle about 3 tablespoons crumb mixture over batter in each pan; swirl mixture with a knife. Spoon remaining batter over crumb mixture. Sprinkle remaining crumb mixture on top. Bake 38 to 43 minutes or until a toothpick inserted in center of bread comes out clean and top is golden brown. Cool in pans 10 minutes. Remove from pans and cool completely on a wire rack.

For gifts with down-home appeal, try sharing our Cinnamon-Carrot Bread — moist, nutty little loaves drizzled with icing — or spicy Candied Apple Butter. The Sweet Felt Stockings *(page 73)* from our Cheery Felt Charmers decorating collection complete the heartwarming offerings.

For icing, combine confectioners sugar, water, and orange extract in a small bowl; stir until smooth. Drizzle icing over bread. Allow icing to harden. Store in an airtight container.
Yield: 4 loaves bread

MAKING PATTERNS

When entire pattern is shown, place tracing paper over pattern and trace pattern; cut out. For a more durable pattern, use a permanent pen to trace pattern onto acetate; cut out.

When only half of pattern is shown (indicated by dashed line on pattern), fold tracing paper in half and place fold along dashed line of pattern. Trace pattern half; turn folded paper over and draw over traced lines on remaining side of paper. Unfold pattern; cut out. For a more durable pattern, use a permanent pen to trace pattern half onto acetate, then turn acetate over and trace pattern half again, aligning dashed lines to form a whole pattern; cut out.

SEWING SHAPES

1. Center pattern on wrong side of 1 fabric piece and use fabric marking pen to draw around pattern. **Do not cut out shape.**
2. Place fabric pieces right sides together. Leaving an opening for turning, carefully sew pieces together **directly on drawn line.**
3. Leaving a 1/4" seam allowance, cut out shape. Clip seam allowance at curves and corners. Turn shape right side out.

MAKING APPLIQUÉS

1. (**Note:** Follow all steps for each appliqué. When tracing patterns for more than 1 appliqué, leave at least 1" between shapes on web. To make a reverse appliqué, trace pattern onto tracing paper, turn traced pattern over, and follow all steps using traced pattern.) Trace appliqué pattern onto paper side of web. Cutting about 1/2" outside drawn lines, cut out web shape.
2. (**Note:** If using a thin fabric for appliqué over a dark or print fabric, fuse interfacing to wrong side of appliqué fabric before completing Step 2.) Fuse web shape to wrong side of appliqué fabric. Cut out shape along drawn lines.

MACHINE APPLIQUÉ

1. Cut a piece of fusible or non-fusible tear-away stabilizer or medium-weight paper slightly larger than design. Fuse or baste stabilizer to wrong side of background fabric under appliqué. Use either regular sewing thread or clear nylon thread for top thread; use thread to match background fabric in bobbin. Set sewing machine for a medium to wide width zigzag stitch. If using clear nylon thread for appliqué, set machine for a short stitch length; for appliqué with regular sewing thread, use a very short stitch length.
2. Beginning on a straight edge of appliqué if possible, position project under presser foot so that most of stitching will be on appliqué. Take a stitch in fabric and bring bobbin thread to top. Hold both threads toward you and sew over them for several stitches to secure. Stitch over all exposed raw edges of appliqué(s) and along detail lines as indicated in instructions.

CROSS STITCH

COUNTED CROSS STITCH (X): Work 1 Cross Stitch for each colored square in chart. For horizontal rows, work stitches in 2 journeys (**Fig. 1**). For vertical rows, complete each stitch as shown in **Fig. 2**. When the chart shows a Backstitch crossing a colored square (**Fig. 3**), work the Cross Stitch first, then work the Backstitch (**Fig. 5**) over the Cross Stitch.

Fig. 1	Fig. 2
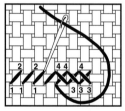	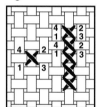

Fig. 3

QUARTER STITCH (1/4X): Quarter stitches are shown as triangular shapes of color in chart and color key. Come up at 1 (**Fig. 4**), then split fabric thread to take needle down at 2.

Fig. 4

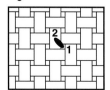

BACKSTITCH (B'ST): For outline details, work Backstitch (shown in chart and color key by black or colored straight lines) after the cross stitch design has been completed (**Fig. 5**).

Fig. 5

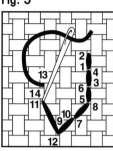

WORKING ON WASTE CANVAS:
1. Cover edges of canvas piece with masking tape.
2. Find desired stitching area on garment and mark center of area with a pin. Match center of canvas to pin. Use blue threads in canvas to place canvas straight on garment; pin canvas to garment. Pin a piece of non-fusible interfacing to wrong side of garment under canvas. Basting through all layers, baste around edges of canvas, from corner to corner, and from side to side.
3. (**Note:** Using a hoop is recommended when working on a large garment. We recommend a hoop that is large enough to encircle entire design.) Using a sharp needle, work design, stitching from large holes to large holes.
4. Remove basting threads and trim canvas to about 3/4" from design. Dampen stitched design. Use tweezers to pull out canvas threads one at a time. Trim interfacing close to design.

EMBROIDERY

STRAIGHT STITCH: Bring needle up at 1 and take needle down at 2 as desired (**Fig. 1**).

Fig. 1

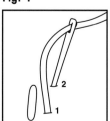

RUNNING STITCH: Make a series of straight stitches with stitch length equal to the space between stitches (**Fig. 2**).

Fig. 2

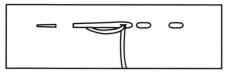

BLANKET STITCH: Referring to **Fig. 3**, bring needle up at 1; keeping thread below point of needle, take needle down at 2 and bring needle up at 3. Continue as shown in **Fig. 4**.

Fig. 3

Fig. 4

OVERCAST STITCH: Referring to **Fig. 5**, bring needle up at 1; take thread around edge of fabric and bring needle up at 2. Continue stitching along edge of fabric.

Fig. 5

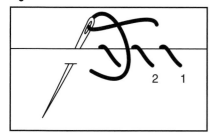

FRENCH KNOT: Bring needle up at 1. Wrap floss once around needle and take needle down at 2, holding end of floss with non-stitching fingers (**Fig. 6**). Tighten knot, then pull needle through fabric, holding floss until it must be released. For a larger knot, use more strands; wrap only once.

Fig. 6

STENCILING

1. (**Note:** These instructions are written for stenciling multicolor designs. For single-color designs, make 1 stencil for entire design.) For first stencil, cut a piece of acetate 1" larger on all sides than entire design. Center acetate over pattern and use pen to trace outlines of all areas of first color in stencil cutting key. For placement guidelines, outline remaining colored areas using dashed lines. Using a new piece of acetate for each additional color in stencil cutting key, repeat for remaining stencils.

2. Place each acetate piece on cutting mat and use craft knife to cut out stencil along solid lines, making sure edges are smooth.

3. Hold or tape first stencil in place. Use a clean, dry stencil brush or sponge piece for each paint color. Dip brush or sponge piece in paint; remove excess on paper towel. Beginning at edge of cutout area, apply paint in a stamping motion over stencil. Repeat until all areas of first stencil have been painted. Carefully remove stencil and allow paint to dry.

4. Using stencils in order indicated in key and matching guidelines on stencils to previously stenciled areas, repeat Step 3 for remaining stencils. To stencil a design in reverse, clean stencils and turn stencils over.

5. For a design stenciled on a garment, follow paint manufacturer's instructions to heat-set design.

PAINTING TECHNIQUES

PREPARING PROJECT
If painting on a garment, wash, dry, and press garment according to paint manufacturer's recommendations. Insert T-shirt form or cardboard covered with waxed paper into garment or under fabric.

TRANSFERRING PATTERN
Trace pattern onto tracing paper. Using removable tape, tape pattern to project. Place transfer paper coated side down between project and tracing paper (using old transfer paper will help prevent smudges). If transferring pattern onto a dark surface, use dressmakers' tracing paper to transfer pattern. Use a stylus to transfer outlines of basecoat areas of design to project (an old ball point pen that does not write makes a good stylus;

press lightly to avoid smudges and heavy lines that are difficult to cover). If necessary, use a soft eraser to remove any smudges.

PAINTING BASECOATS
(**Note:** A disposable plate makes a good palette.) Use a medium round brush for large areas and a small round brush for small areas. Do not overload brush. It is better to apply several thin coats of paint than to have brushmarks. Let paint dry between coats.

TRANSFERRING DETAILS
To transfer detail lines to design, replace pattern and transfer paper over painted basecoats and use stylus to lightly transfer detail lines onto project.

PAINTING DETAILS
Sideloading (shading and highlighting): Dip 1 corner of a flat brush in water; blot on paper towel. Dip dry corner of brush into paint. Stroke brush back and forth on palette until there is a gradual change from paint to water in each brushstroke. Stroke loaded side of brush along detail line on project, pulling brush toward you and turning project if necessary. For shading, sideload brush with darker color of paint. For highlighting, sideload brush with lighter color of paint.
Linework: Let paint dry before beginning linework to avoid smudging lines or ruining pen. Draw over detail lines with permanent pen.
Dots: Dip the tip of a round paintbrush, the handle end of a paintbrush, or 1 end of a toothpick in paint and touch to project. Dip in paint each time for uniform dots.
Sponge painting: Lightly dampen sponge piece. Dip sponge piece into paint and blot on paper towel to remove excess paint. Use a stamping motion to apply paint. Reapply paint to sponge as necessary.

FINISHING PROJECT
Remove T-shirt form or cardboard from garment or fabric. For designs painted on a garment with acrylic paint, either follow manufacturer's instructions to heat-set design or place garment on a protected ironing board and use a hot iron to press on wrong side. For projects which also use dimensional paint, heat-set design before applying dimensional paint.

(Continued on page 160)

WOODBURNING

Caution: Follow manufacturer's instructions when using a woodburning pen. Allow the pen and point to cool completely before changing points.

Practice woodburning techniques on a wood scrap until you are able to control direction and thickness of lines and make curves, dots, or triangles. The darkness of the woodburned design is determined by the speed of the moving pen, not the wattage of the pen or the pressure applied. The slower the pen is moved, the darker the design.

We used a universal point (a wedge shaped tip with flat sides) and a flow point (a rounded tip) to make the woodburned projects in this book. Most woodburning pens come with a universal point. Other optional points are available from the manufacturer.

PREPARING PROJECT

Sand project lightly if necessary; wipe with a slightly damp paper towel or tack cloth to remove dust.

TRANSFERRING PATTERN

Trace pattern onto tracing paper. Using removable tape, tape pattern to project. Place transfer paper coated side down between project and tracing paper (using old transfer paper will help prevent smudges). Use a stylus to lightly transfer pattern onto project (an old ball point pen that does not write makes a good stylus). If necessary, use a soft eraser to remove any smudges.

BURNING DESIGN

Straight lines: Using universal point, hold pen at a 45 degree angle to surface with tip of point next to edge of a metal ruler placed along design line; pull pen toward you to burn line. For thicker line, change angle of pen to allow more of the flat side of point to touch wood.

Curved lines: Using either universal or flow point, position tip of point on design line and pull pen toward you, twirling handle of pen slightly in hand to direct curve. Turn project as necessary.

Triangles: Using universal point, hold pen almost parallel to surface and apply flat side of point to wood to burn a triangle. For a triangle border, burn triangles side by side.

CREDITS

We want to extend a warm *thank you* to the generous people who allowed us to photograph our projects in their homes.

- *Sacred Celebration:* Shirley Held
- *For Santa Collectors:* Ron and Becky Werle
- *A Medley of Mantels:* William and Nancy Appleton, William and Isabel Eggart, Leland and Georgiana Gunn, Dick and Jan Henry, and Shirley Held
- *Cheery Felt Charmers:* Carl and Monte Brunck
- *"Bee" Merry:* John and Anne Jarrard
- *A Brown Bag Noel* and *The Sharing of Christmas:* Charles and Peg Mills
- *Gingerbread Party:* Duncan and Nancy Porter

A special thanks also goes to the following businesses for permitting us to photograph projects on their premises: Pinnacle Vista Lodge, 7510 Hwy. 300, Little Rock, Arkansas 72212, *Snowy Mountain Christmas*; Cynthia East Fabrics, Inc., 1523 Rebsamen Park Road, Little Rock, Arkansas 72202, *Santa's Sweetshop*; and Hotze House Bed and Breakfast, 1619 Louisiana Street, Little Rock, Arkansas 72216, "Away in a Manger Mantel" from *A Medley of Mantels.*

We would like to recognize Viking Husqvarna Sewing Machine Company of Cleveland, Ohio, for providing the sewing machines used to make many of our projects.

To Magna IV Color Imaging of Little Rock, Arkansas, we say thank you for the superb color reproduction and excellent pre-press preparation.

Our sincere appreciation goes to photographers Ken West, Larry Pennington, Mark Mathews, Karen Shirey, and David Hale of Peerless Photography, Little Rock, Arkansas; and Jerry R. Davis of Jerry Davis Photography, Little Rock, Arkansas, for their time, patience, and excellent work.

To the talented people who helped in the creation of the following projects in this book, we extend a special word of thanks.

- *Frosty Fellow Stitched Vest*, page 105: Susan Fouts (needlework adaptation by Jane Chandler)
- *Jolly Santa Sweatshirt*, page 110: Deborah Lambein

We are sincerely grateful to the people who assisted in making and testing the projects in this book: Lois Allen, Pamela S. Nash, and Debra Smith.